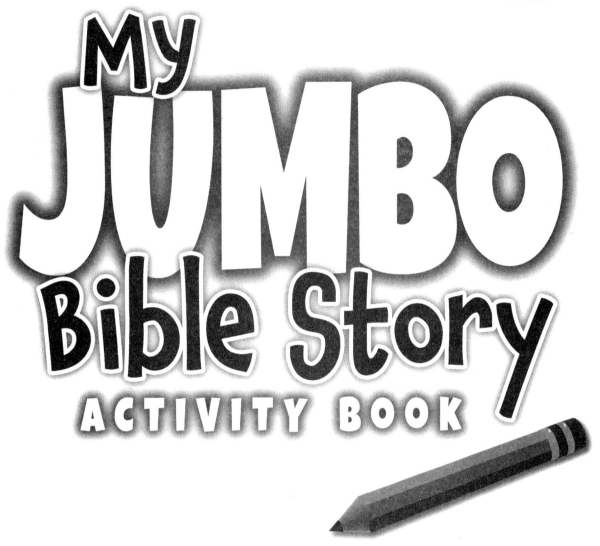

My JUMBO Bible Story ACTIVITY BOOK

Illustrated by Michael Denman

warner press KiDs

305800211952

God Creates the World (From Genesis 1:1—2:3)

Long, long ago, there was no world. Everything was dark.
Then God said something. What was it?

Use the code to find out.

GENESIS 1:3

CODE:

B = 🔆 H = ☀ L = 🔦 T = 💡

R = ⭐ E = 🕯 G = 🔥 I = 🌙

Each day God added something new to His beautiful world.

Draw a line to match the opposites.

God worked for six days to create everything.
Last, He made a man and woman, Adam and Eve.

Circle the hidden pictures: apple, snake, leaf, Bible, cross, bird, fish, flower

On the seventh day God rested. He wants us to rest too.

Draw a picture of how you rest.

The Wedding Miracle (From John 2:1-11)

Jesus, His mother, and the disciples had all been invited to a wedding.

Help them reach the wedding.

START

During the party, the family ran out of something. What was it?

Follow the lines from the letters to the boxes. Then write the letters.

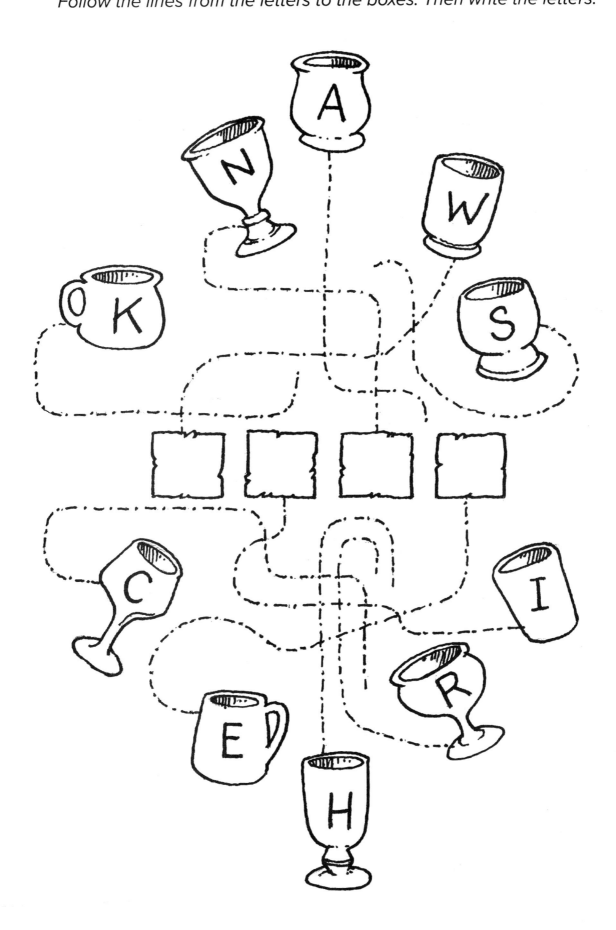

Jesus' mother told the servants to do what Jesus said.
Jesus told them to fill six large jars with water. So they did. *Connect the dots.*

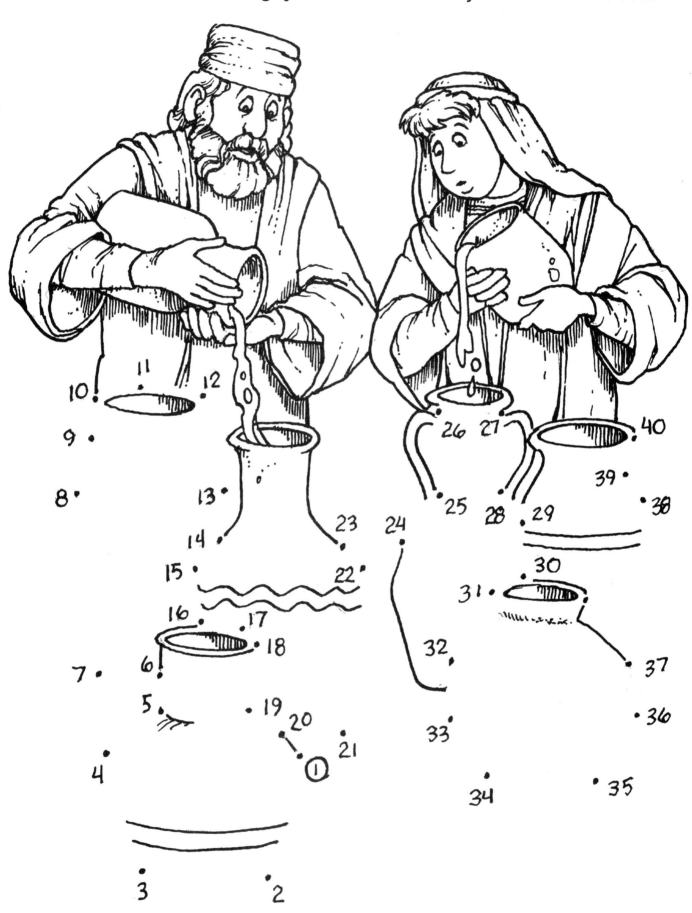

Jesus changed the water into wine.
The man in charge of the party told the bridegroom, "Usually people serve good wine first, then cheap wine." What did he say next?

Use the code to find out.

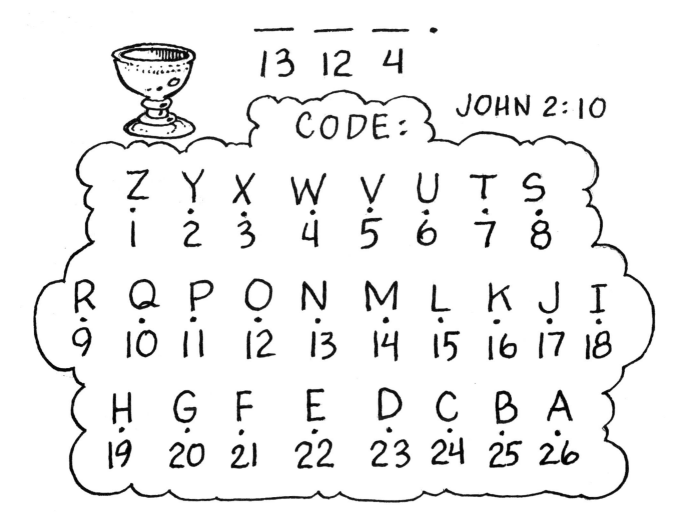

2 12 6   19 26 5 22

8 26 5 22 23   7 19 22

25 22 8 7   7 18 15 15

13 12 4 .

CODE: JOHN 2:10

Z Y X W V U T S
1 2 3 4 5 6 7 8

R Q P O N M L K J I
9 10 11 12 13 14 15 16 17 18

H G F E D C B A
19 20 21 22 23 24 25 26

Cain and Abel (From Genesis 4:1-16)

Cain and Abel were the first children. Cain was a farmer, and Abel was a shepherd.

Draw Cain's hoe and Abel's sheep.

Each brother brought God an offering. God was proud of Abel,
but He was not happy with Cain. This made Cain very mad! What did God say?

Write the words in the shapes that match.

are you
?
If you
what is
will be
.

From Genesis 4:6

do
Why
accepted
you
right
angry

Cain didn't want to do what God said.
Instead, he said to Abel, "Let's go out to the field." Then what did Cain do?
Write the first letter of each picture in the boxes to find out.

God made Cain leave his home and family.
He had to move far away and live a very hard life because of what he'd done.

Help Cain reach the land of Nod.

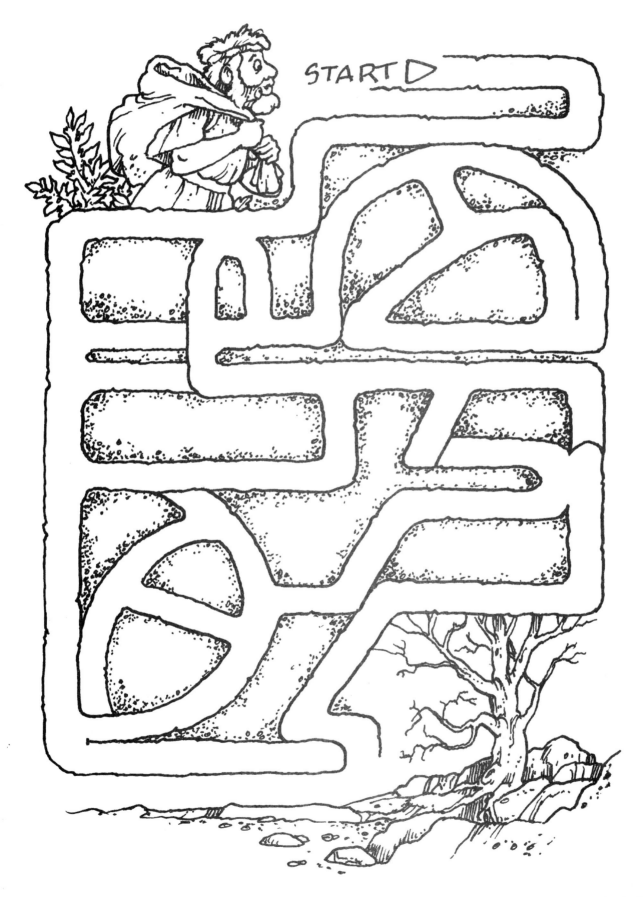

START ▷

The Woman at the Well (From John 4:1-43)

Jesus was traveling through Samaria. He was very tired and sat by a well to rest.

Which path will take Jesus to the well?

A woman came to the well, and Jesus asked her for a drink. She wanted regular water, but Jesus said she could have living water and eternal life.

Circle the hidden pictures: jug, cup, frog, Bible, cross, raindrop, boat, ant

Jesus knew all about the woman, even though He had never met her before. What did she say?

Write the letter that comes BEFORE the letter under the line to find out.

‾ ‾ ‾ ‾ ‾ ‾ ‾
J D B O T F F

‾ ‾ ‾ ‾ ‾ ‾ ‾
U I B U Z P V

‾ ‾ ‾ ‾
B S F B

‾ ‾ ‾ ‾ ‾ ‾ ‾ ‾ .
Q S P Q I F U

JOHN 4:19

ABCDEFGHIJKLM
NOPQRSTUVWXYZ

Jesus told her He was the Messiah. The woman left her water jar and ran to tell everyone in town. Then Jesus taught the people, and many believed in Him.

Help the woman reach the town.

START ▷

Noah and the Flood (From Genesis 6:9—9:17)

One day God told Noah to build an ark.
God was going to send a flood to cover the earth.

Put an X on 5 things that do not belong in the picture.

God told Noah to take his family and two of every kind of animal on the ark.
God would keep them safe. *Find and circle the animal names.*

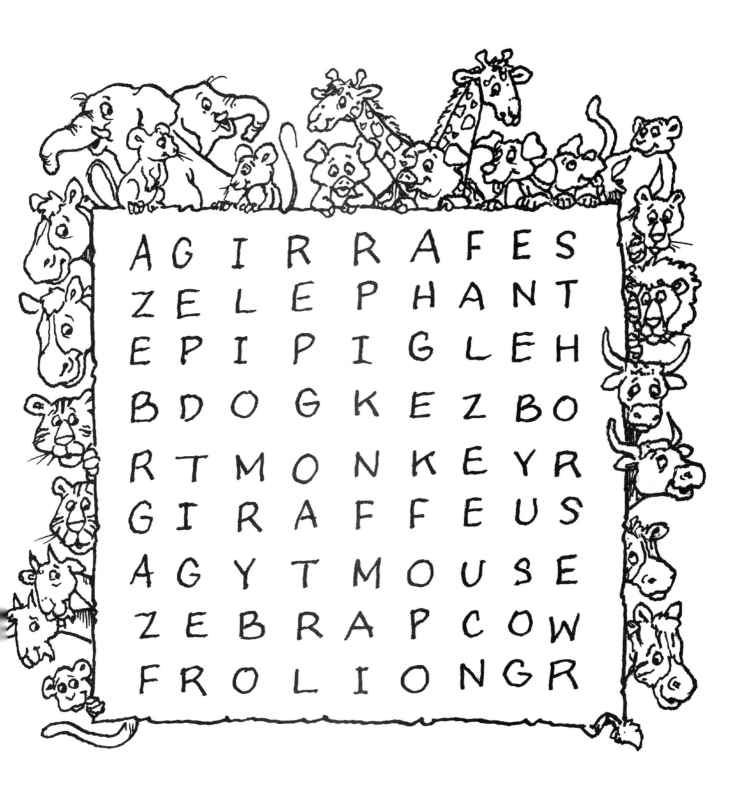

```
A G I R R A F E S
Z E L E P H A N T
E P I P I G L E H
B D O G K E Z B O
R T M O N K E Y R
G I R A F F E U S
A G Y T M O U S E
Z E B R A P C O W
F R O L I O N G R
```

Soon, the rain came pouring down. How many days and nights did it rain?

Follow the lines from the letters to the boxes. Then write the letters.

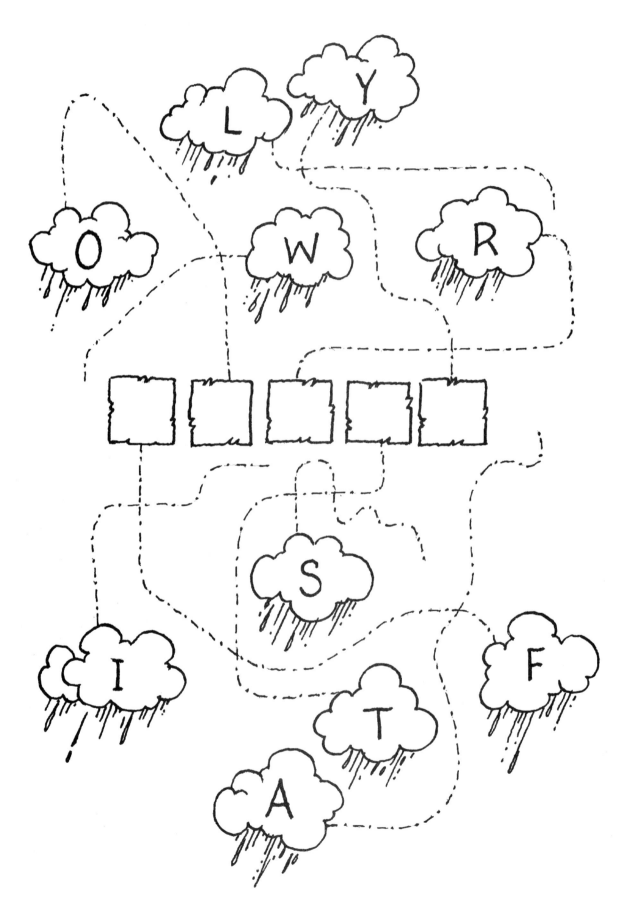

At last, the flood dried up, and everyone came out of the ark. Then God put a rainbow in the sky. He promised Noah never to flood the whole earth again.

Connect the dots.

Jesus Heals a Leper (From Luke 5:12-16)

One day a man came to Jesus. He had a bad skin disease called leprosy.

Draw bandages over the man's sores.

The leper knew Jesus could heal him. "Lord, if You are willing,
You can make me clean," the man begged. What did Jesus say?

Use the code to find out.

LUKE 5:13

CODE:

A = 🍎 B = 🐻 C = ⭐

E = ◯ G = 🍀 I = 🐰 L = ♡

M = 🌙 N = 🐟 W = ☀

Right away, the man's leprosy was gone! Jesus said, "Don't tell anyone."
What did Jesus want the man to do?

Cross out every Z. Then write the letters you have left in order on the lines.

___ ___ ___ ___ ___ ___

___ ___ ___ ___ ___ ___ ___

___ ___ ___ ___ ___ ___ ___ .

LUKE
5:14

The man couldn't keep the good news to himself. Soon, crowds came to hear Jesus and be healed. But Jesus would often go to quiet places to pray.

Help Jesus find the path to a quiet place.

Happy Valentine's Day! (From John 3:16)

Valentine's Day is a time to thank God for the ones we love. Who do you love?

Finish drawing the faces.

Lots of people love you too!

Find and circle the names of people in your family.
Then write the letters you have left in order on the lines.

J G R A N D M A
B R O T H E R E
A S I S T E R S
U G R A N D P A
N U M O M D A D
T S U N C L E

Who loves you most of all?

_ _ _ _ _ _

The Bible tells us how much God loves us.

Write the words in the shapes that match to read the verse.

For ⭐ so ♥ the ⬤ that he 🕊 his one and only ◆.

John 3:16

world   God   Son

loved   gave

Color this Valentine and give it to someone special!

God Tests Abraham (From Genesis 22:1-19)

One day God asked Abraham to do a hard thing.
"Offer your son, Isaac, as a sacrifice to me," God said.

Help Abraham and Isaac reach the mountain.

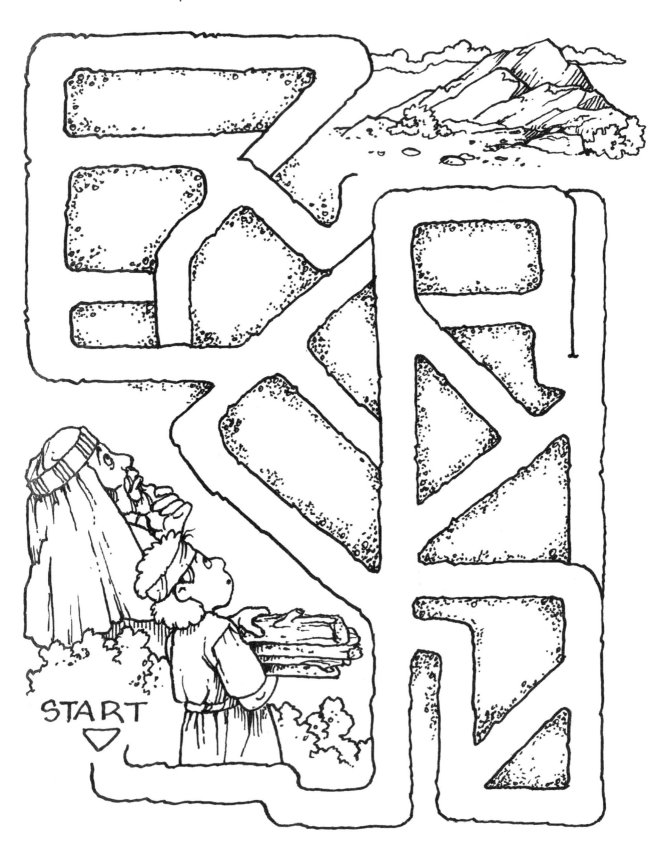

START

Isaac carried the firewood up the mountain.
He asked his dad, "Where is the lamb for the offering?"

Circle the hidden pictures: fire, knife, lamb, donkey, Bible, cross, nut, apple

Abraham loved his son so much.
He also loved and trusted God. What did he tell Isaac?
Use the code to find out.

G O D W I L L
13 4 7 20 17 23 23

P R O V I D E
6 10 4 18 17 7 9

T H E L A M B.
14 15 9 23 1 25 3

GENESIS 22:8

CODE:

A	B	C	D	E	F	G	H
1	3	5	7	9	11	13	15

I	J	K	L	M	N	O	P	Q	R
17	19	21	23	25	2	4	6	8	10

S	T	U	V	W	X	Y	Z
12	14	16	18	20	22	24	26

God never wanted Abraham to hurt Isaac. God only wanted to see if Abraham would obey. God gave them a ram to sacrifice instead. Then He blessed Abraham.

Draw a picture of the ram in the bushes.

A Woman Anoints Jesus' Feet (From Luke 7:36-50)

Jesus was having dinner at Simon's house.
A woman came in with something in her hands. What was it?

Color the spaces with dots to see the picture.

The woman cried on Jesus' feet and wiped them with her hair. Then she poured perfume on them. She was so sorry for bad things she had done.

Put an X on 5 things that do not belong in the picture.

**Jesus knew Simon thought the woman was bad. Jesus said,
"You did not wash My feet, but this woman washed them with tears."
A good host would have washed Jesus' feet to welcome Him.**

Connect the dots.

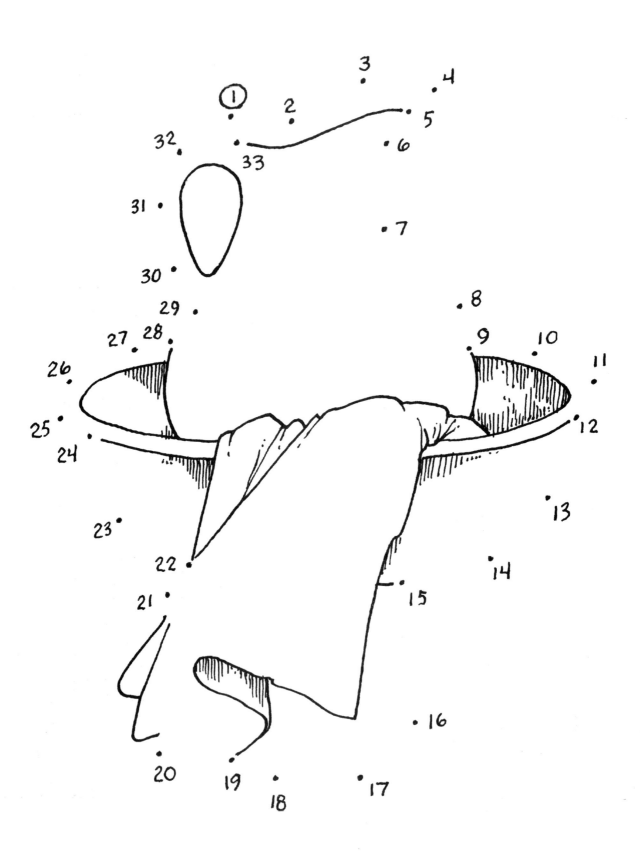

Jesus knew the woman was truly sorry for her sins. What did He tell her?

Write the letter that comes BEFORE the letter under the line to find out.

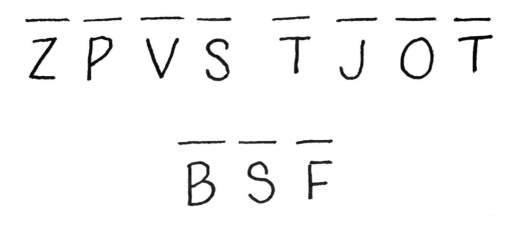

‾ ‾ ‾ ‾   ‾ ‾ ‾ ‾
Z P V S   T J O T

‾ ‾ ‾
B S F

‾ ‾ ‾ ‾ ‾ ‾ ‾ .
G P S H J W F O

LUKE 7:48

ABCDEFGHIJKLM
NOPQRSTUVWXYZ

Jacob and Esau (From Genesis 25:21–34)

Isaac and Rebekah had wanted a baby for a long time.
Isaac prayed, and God sent them something special. What was it?

Follow the lines from the letters to the boxes. Then write the letters.

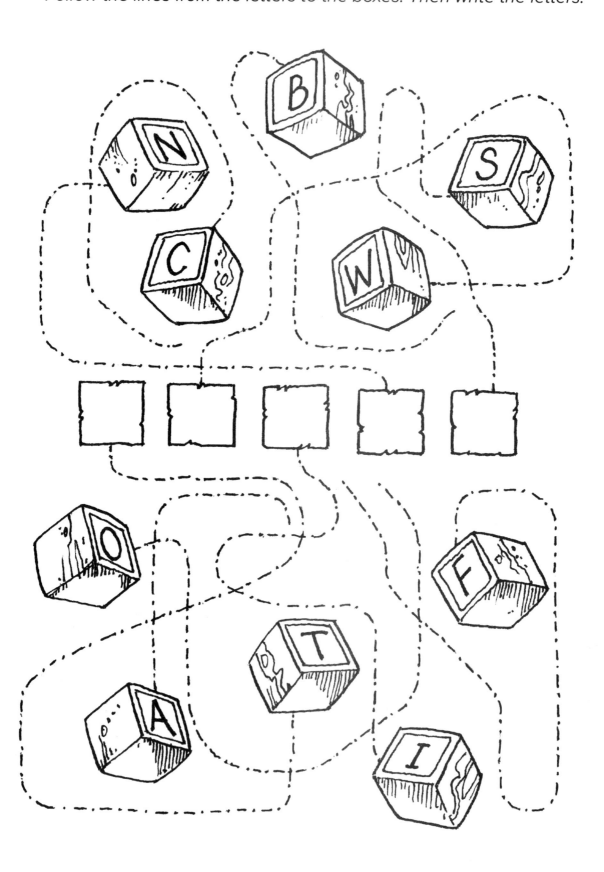

When the boys grew up, Esau became a good hunter. Jacob liked to stay home.
Connect the dots.

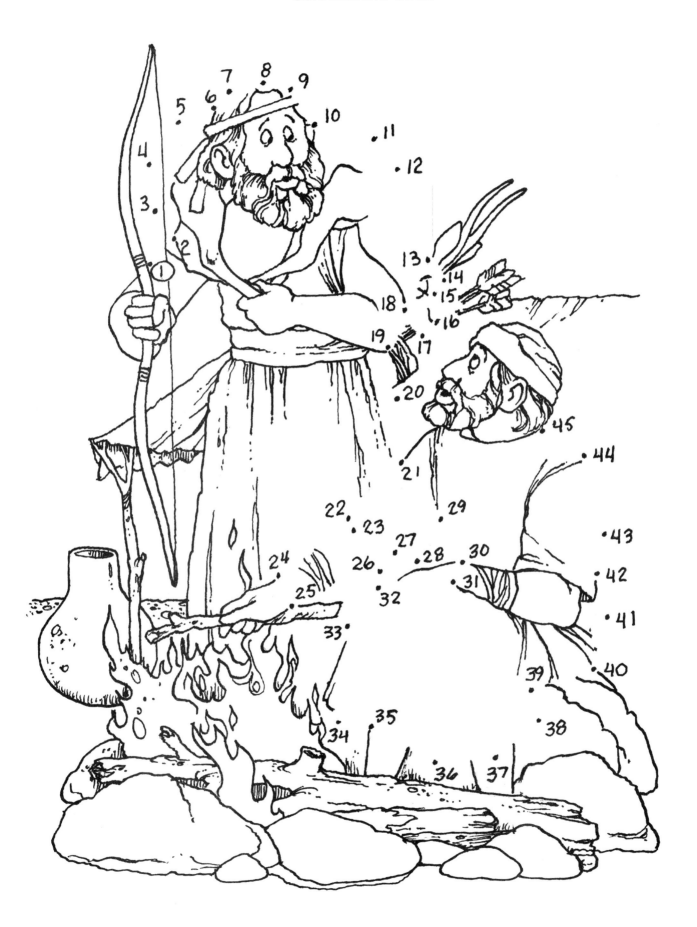

**Jacob was cooking when Esau came home from hunting.
"I'm starving!" said Esau. Then what did he say?**

Write the first letter of each picture in the boxes to find out.

(FROM GENESIS 25:30)

Jacob said, "I will if you give me your birthright." Esau did, and Jacob got Esau's special place in the family. Have you ever made a poor choice?

Draw a picture or write about it.

Joseph's Special Coat (From Genesis 37)

Joseph was Jacob's favorite son.
Jacob gave him a special coat because he loved him.

Look carefully at the two coats. Circle the things that are different.

Joseph's brothers were jealous. And when Joseph dreamed he was better than them, they hated him even more! *Draw faces on Joseph and his brothers.*

One day, the brothers were watching sheep. They saw Joseph coming.
"Let's get rid of him!" they said. They took his coat and threw him in a dry well.

Circle the hidden pictures: sun, moon, star, goat, sheep, Bible, cross, banana

The brothers put blood on the coat. Then they gave it to their dad. "My son is dead!" Jacob cried. What had the brothers really done with him?

Use the code to find out.

THEY SOLD

HIM AS

A SLAVE.

CODE:

A B C D E F G H
26 25 24 23 22 21 20 19

I J K L M N O P Q R
18 17 16 15 14 13 12 11 10 9

S T U V W X Y Z
8 7 6 5 4 3 2 1

Jesus Comes to Jerusalem (From Luke 19:28-40)

When Jesus was almost to Jerusalem, He asked His disciples to get something.
What was it? *Connect the dots.*

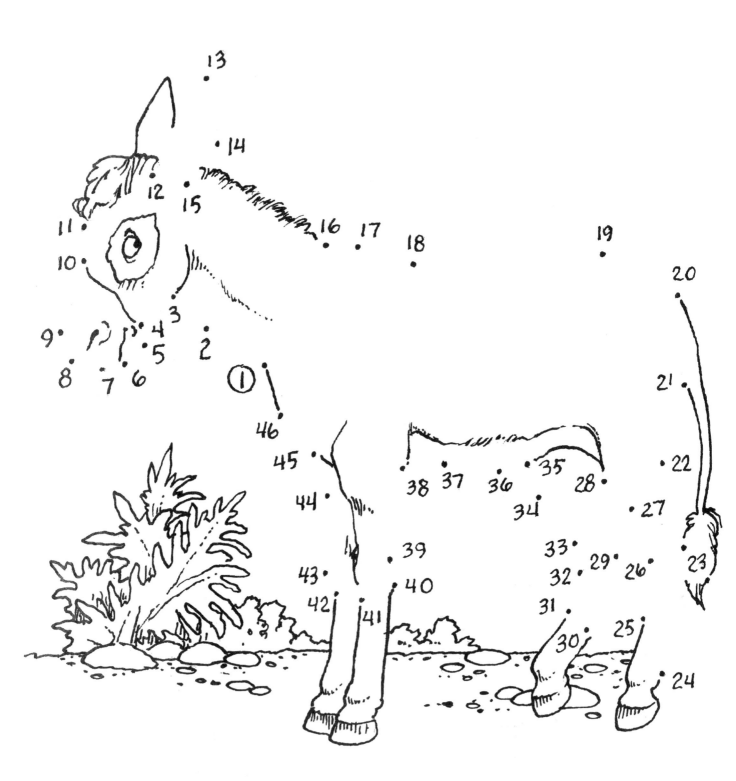

People were so happy to see Jesus.
They waved palm branches to welcome Him to town.

Help Jesus reach Jerusalem.

Then the people started shouting joyful praise to God. What did they say?

Use the secret code to find out.

IS THE

IN THE

OF THE ____!

CODE: LUKE 19:38

A = △   B = □   C = ☺   D = ♡   E = ♪

G = 🌳   H = 🐰   I = 🍎   K = 👑   L = 🦁   M = 🍀

N = 🎵   O = ☆   R = ⚡   S = 🪁   W = 🌙

**Some bad men didn't want people to praise Jesus. They said,
"Tell them to be quiet!" But Jesus said, "If they are quiet, the stones will cry out."**

Draw faces on the stones, so they can shout praise to God!

The Easter Story (From Luke 23:44—24:12)

It was daytime, but the sky was as dark as night. People were sad and crying.
God's Son Jesus had died.

Color in the spaces with dots to see the picture.

A good man took Jesus' body and put it in a new tomb.
Then a huge rock was rolled in front of the door.

Circle the hidden pictures: dove, lily, Bible, cross, perfume bottle, grapes, cup, turtle

Women came to the **tomb**. The **stone** was **rolled** away, and **Jesus** was not there!
An **angel** said, "**He** has **risen!**"

Find and circle the underlined words in the puzzle.

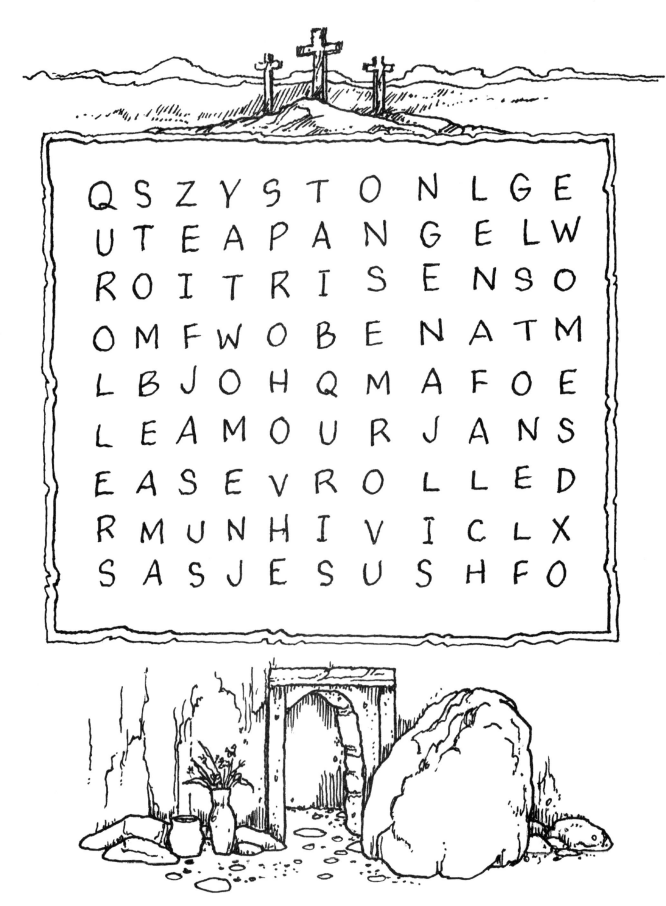

```
Q S Z Y S T O N L G E
U T E A P A N G E L W
R O I T R I S E N S O
O M F W O B E N A T M
L B J O H Q M A F O E
L E A M O U R J A N S
E A S E V R O L L E D
R M U N H I V I C L X
S A S J E S U S H F O
```

**Then the women ran to tell the disciples the good news.
Jesus is alive! Who will you tell about Jesus this Easter?**

Draw that person here.

Moses and the 10 Commandments (From Exodus 19—20)

God said, "Moses, tell the people I am coming to the mountain to give them a message." What was the name of the mountain?

Write the first letter of each picture to find out.

Then Moses climbed the mountain to talk with God.

Circle the hidden pictures: pen, trumpet, fire, cross, Bible, cloud, flower, arrow

The people were afraid of the smoke, thunder, and lightning.
They heard a loud trumpet while God and Moses talked.

Draw the clouds of smoke on the mountain. Draw lightning in the sky.

God gave Moses 10 Commandments, or laws, for the people to live by.
What was the first commandment? *Use the code to find out.*

__ __ __ __ __ __ __ __
23 3 15 11 16 2 24 24

__ __ __ __ __ __
16 2 17 10 1 3

__ __ __ __ __ __ __ __ __
3 13 16 10 9 14 3 8 11

__ __ __ __ __ __ __ __ .
4 10 12 3 9 10 26 10

EXODUS 20:3

CODE:
A B C D E F G H I J K L M N O P Q
2· 4· 6· 8·10·12· 14· 16·18· 20· 22·24· 26· 1· 3· 5·7
R S T U V W X Y Z
9· 11· 13·15· 17· 19· 21· 23·25

The Parable of the Weeds (From Matthew 13:24-30)

Jesus told a story about a farmer who planted good wheat seed in his field.

Put an X on 5 things that do not belong in the picture.

While the farmer slept, a bad man threw weed seeds in the field. The weeds grew with the farmer's wheat.

Find the path that will lead the bad man to the field.

When harvest time came, servants pulled the weeds.
Then they put the wheat safely in the farmer's **barn.** *Connect the dots.*

Jesus is like the farmer, and we are His good wheat.
If we believe in Him, we will go to heaven someday.
Draw what you think heaven will be like.

Hannah's Prayer (From 1 Samuel 1:1-20)

Hannah cried and cried. "Why are you so sad?" her husband asked.
What was the matter? *Use the code to find out.*

Hannah went to the temple. Eli the priest saw her crying and praying there.

Help Hannah find her way to the temple.

START ▷

Eli asked her what was wrong.
When she told him, he said, "May God give you what you have asked for."

Circle the hidden pictures:
baby bottle, teddy bear, pacifier, spoon, Bible, bowl, star, cross

Soon, God answered Hannah's prayer. She had a sweet baby boy named Samuel.

Connect the dots.

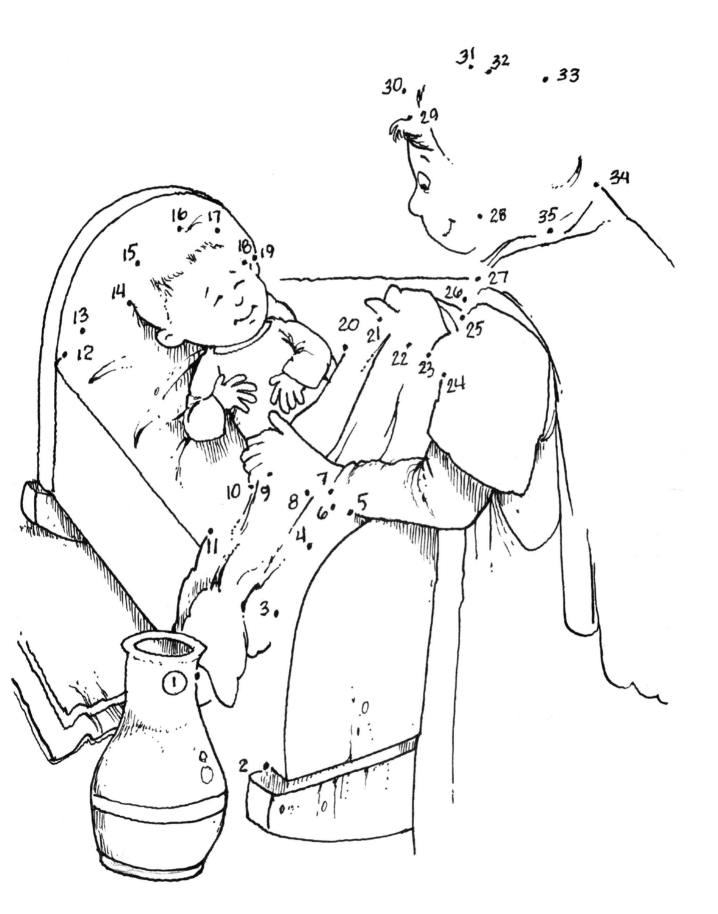

Jesus Calms the Storm (From Mark 4:35-41)

Jesus had been teaching, and He was tired.
"Let's go to the other side of the lake," He said.

Which path leads to the boat?

A big storm came. Waves were crashing over the boat!
But Jesus was sound asleep on a pillow.

Put an X on 5 things that are wrong with the picture.

The **disciples** woke Jesus up. "Don't you care if we <u>drown</u>?" they asked.
<u>Jesus</u> said to the wind and the <u>waves</u>, "Quiet. Be <u>still</u>."
The <u>wind</u> died down, and it was completely <u>calm</u>.
(From Mark 4:38-39)

Find and circle the underlined words in the puzzle.

```
S O V E S T I L J O
T D I S C I P L E S
I R A T O X B Y S U
L O P I T C K Q U P
L W I N D O E U S O
R N A C A L M I J U
O I G H N M A E E D
T C W A V E S T S A
G L A R I L C L U F
```

The disciples were afraid!
They had never known anyone who could do what Jesus did. What did they say?
Write the letter that comes BEFORE the letter under the line to find out.

F W F O U I F

X J O E B O E

U I F

X B W F T

P C F Z I J N .

MARK 4:41

A B C D E F G H I J K L M
N O P Q R S T U V W X Y Z

Samson (From Judges 13—16)

God made Samson very strong, so he could fight Israel's enemies.

Draw Samson's muscles and long hair.

One day, a wild animal jumped out at Samson. Samson killed it with his bare hands!

Color in the spaces with dots to see the animal.

Samson fell in love with Delilah. She begged him to tell the secret of his strength. At last, he did. What was the secret?

Write the words in the shapes that match.

IF YOU [✂] MY [🌫],

MY [🪮] WILL [♡],

AND I WILL BECOME [🔍].

(FROM JUDGES 16:17)

WEAK   CUT   STRENGTH

LEAVE   HAIR

Bad men cut his hair and put him in jail. Samson asked God
for help. Then his hair grew, his strength came back,
and he defeated the enemy.

Circle the hidden pictures: scissors, fox, bee, Bible, brush, comb, cross, rope

Happy Mother's Day! (From Proverbs 31:10-31)

The Bible tells some of the great things moms do.
They take good care of their families!

Draw a line to match the pictures.

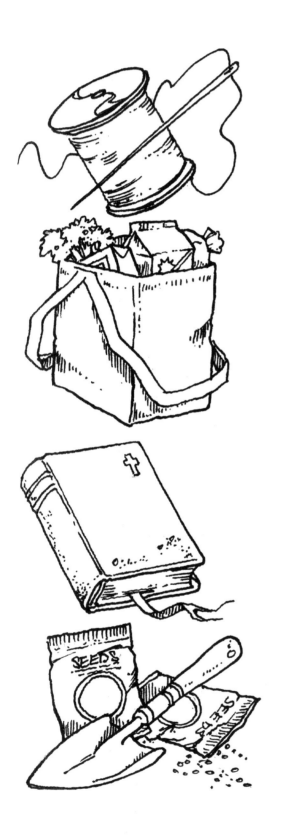

Moms hold us when we are babies. They teach us when we are kids. They are proud of us when we are all grown up.

Write 1, 2, 3, 4 on the pictures to put them in the right order.

Moms need to hear us say, "Thank you! Great job!"
Kind words show moms we love them! What does the Bible say?

Cross out every Zz. Then write the letters you have left on the lines to find out.

PROVERBS
31: 31

What makes your mom special?

Write words that describe your mom on the petals.
Then color the picture and give it to her.

David and Goliath (From 1 Samuel 17:1-50)

One day, David went to visit his brothers at the battlefield.

Help David find his way to his brothers.

**Someone was shouting at the soldiers. "Who will fight me?" he yelled.
"I will," David said. Who was shouting?**

Follow the lines from the letters to the boxes. Then write the letters.

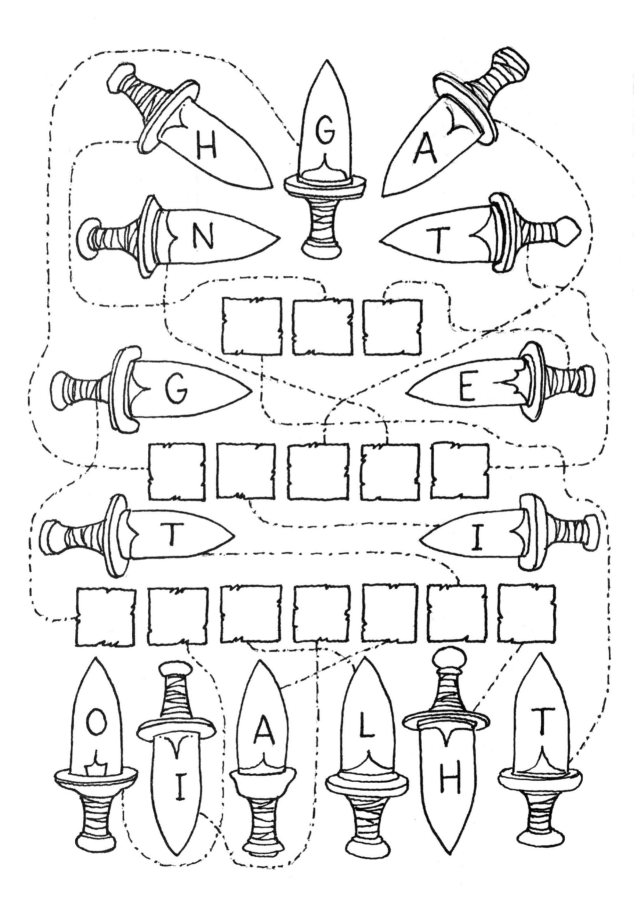

David went to a stream and found 5 smooth stones. Then he went to fight the giant.

Circle 5 stones hidden in the picture.

David slung a stone, and it hit Goliath on the forehead.
Down he crashed! David knew who had helped him kill the giant. What did he say?

Use the code to find out.

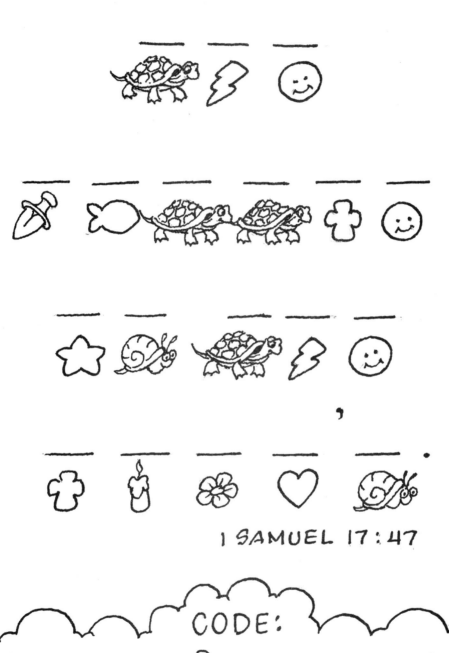

THE

BATTLE

IS THE ,

LORD'S .

1 SAMUEL 17:47

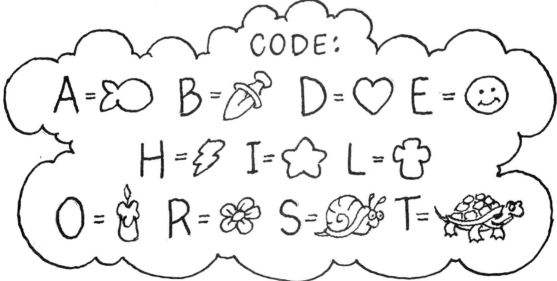

CODE:
A = 🐟 B = 🔩 D = ♡ E = ☺
H = ⚡ I = ☆ L = ✚
O = 🕯 R = ✿ S = 🐌 T = 🐢

Jesus Heals a Wild Man (From Mark 5:1-20)

A wild man lived in a graveyard. He had an evil spirit, and no one could help him.

Connect the dots.

When the wild man saw Jesus, he ran to Him. Jesus knew the man needed help.
What did He say to the evil spirit?

Write the letter that comes AFTER the letter under the line to find out.

B N L D   N T S

N E

S G H R L A M !

MARK 5:8

A B C D E F G H I J K L M
N O P Q R S T U V W X Y Z

A herd of pigs was eating on the hill.
The evil spirit asked if it could be sent into the pigs. Jesus agreed.

Put an X on 5 things that are wrong with the picture.

**The wild man was so happy to be well! Jesus said,
"Go home and tell everyone what has happened to you."**

Who can you tell about Jesus? Draw a picture here.

Elisha and the Widow's Oil (From 2 Kings 4:1-7)

One day, a poor widow came to Elisha for help.

Which path will take her to Elisha?

Some bad things happened to her family. What were they?

Write the words in the shapes that match.

HER ⬭ 🏺.

SHE COULDN'T ▭ HER 🏺.

HER 🏺 WERE GOING TO

BE 🏺.

PAY • DIED • SONS • HUSBAND

SLAVES • BILLS

All the widow had was a little jar of oil. Elisha told her
to ask the neighbors for all of their empty jars.

How many jars can you find hidden in the picture? _____

The widow's <u>oil</u> did not stop <u>pouring</u> until every <u>jar</u> was <u>filled</u>.
<u>Elisha</u> had done a <u>miracle</u>! He told her to <u>sell</u> the oil, pay her <u>bills</u>,
and take care of her <u>sons</u>.

Write the underlined words where they fit in the puzzle.
Some letters are given to help you.

Who Is Jesus? (From Matthew 16:13-20)

One day Jesus and His disciples were walking to a city in the north.

Help them reach the city.

START ▷

"Who do people say I am?" Jesus asked. What did the disciples say?

Write the words in the shapes that match.

Some say ☐☐☐ the ☐☐☐☐☐☐. Others say ☐☐☐☐☐ or ☐☐☐☐☐☐☐☐ or one of the other ☐☐☐☐☐☐☐.

From Matthew 16:14

Jeremiah

Baptist

Elijah   John

prophets

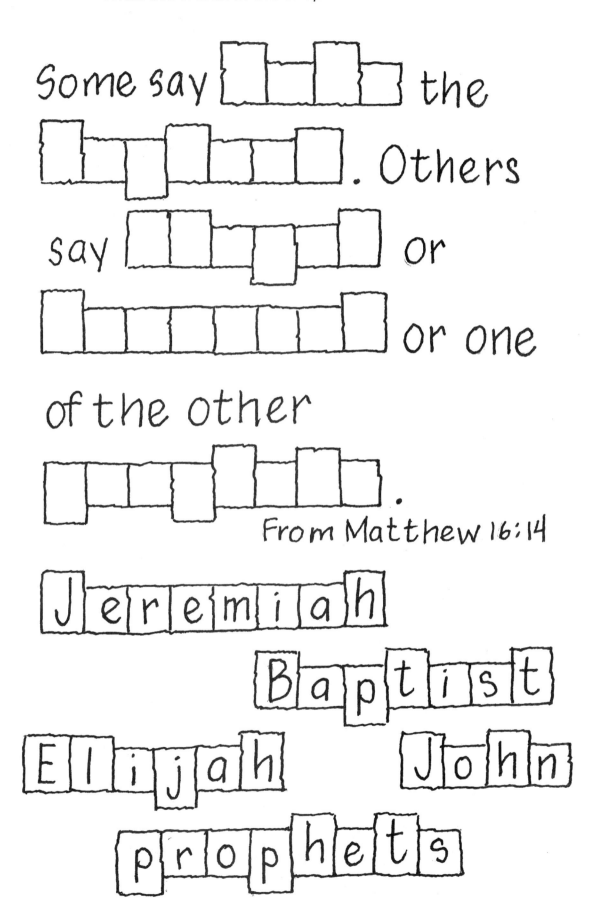

__ __ __   __ __ __ __ __ __
3 23 11   26 17 18 13 12 18

__ __ __ __ __ __ __ ,
2 18 15 15 10 26 12

__ __ __ __ __ __ __ __
13 12 18 15 23 25 23 16

__ __ __ __ __ __ __ __ __
13 12 18 4 10 9 10 25 14

__ __ __ .   MATTHEW 16:16
14 23 20

CODE:

Z	Y	X	W	V	U	T	S	R	Q	P	O	N
1	3	5	7	9	11	13	15	17	19	21	23	25

M	L	K	J	I	H	G	F	E	D	C	B	A
2	4	6	8	10	12	14	16	18	20	22	24	26

Jesus said, "You are Peter, and on this rock I will build my church." Later on, Peter would tell others about Jesus and teach them how to be Christians.

Draw a picture of your church here.

A Slave Girl Helps Naaman (From 2 Kings 5:1-15)

Naaman, a great leader and soldier, had a BIG problem. He had a bad skin disease called leprosy. Draw leprosy on Naaman's arms and legs.

Naaman's wife had a little slave girl. The girl said,
"The prophet in Israel could cure Naaman's leprosy."
So Naaman went to Elisha's house.

Help Naaman reach Elisha's house.

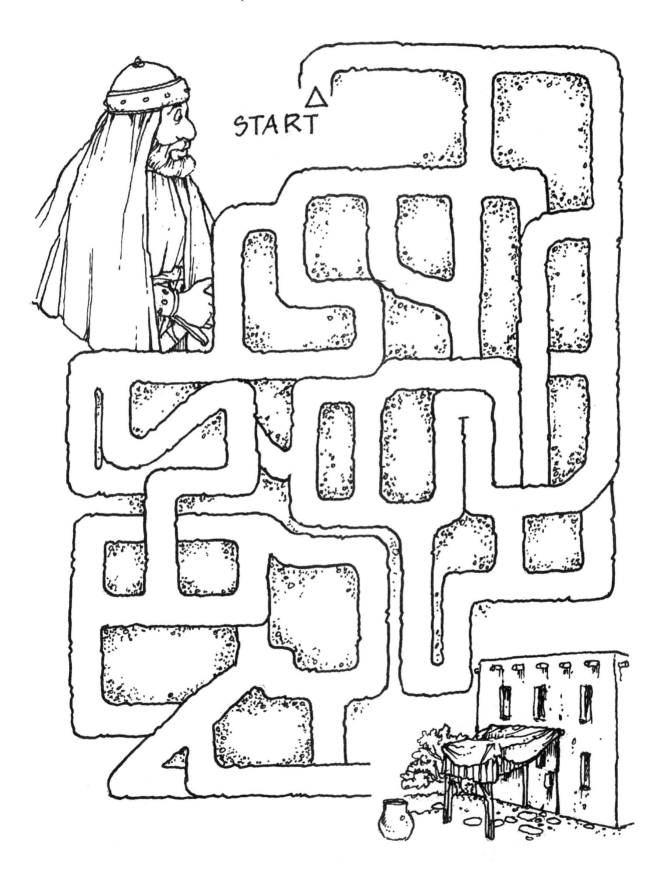

START

Elisha told Naaman if he would wash in the Jordan River he would be healed.
How many times did Naaman have to wash?

Color in the spaces with dots to find out.

Naaman did not want to obey Elisha, but he did.
When he came out of the water the last time, his leprosy was gone!

Circle the hidden pictures: bandage, cane, Bible, fish, turtle, cross, bar of soap, towel

Happy Father's Day! (From Proverbs 23:22)

Father's Day is a great time to tell dads how special they are.
They work hard for their families!

Draw a line to match the pictures.

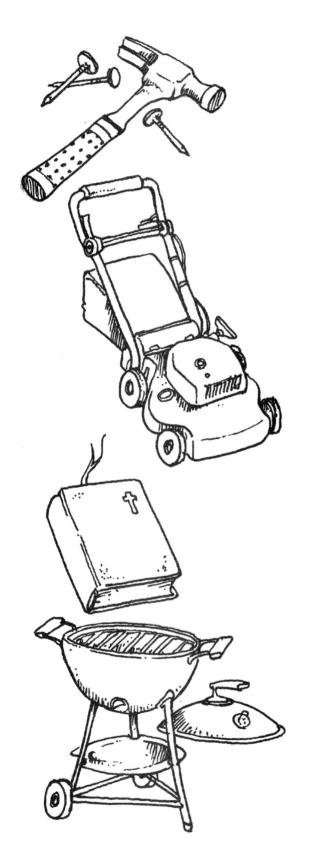

Dads enjoy spending time with their kids. Some like to play games or sports. Some like to play music or read books. But dads always know how to have fun!

Put an X on 5 things that do not belong in the picture.

Dads teach us how to obey God, so we can have a happy life.
What does the Bible say we should do?

Cross out every Zz. Then write the letters you have left on the lines to find out.

__ __ __ __ __ __

__ __ __ __ __

__ __ __ __ __ ,

__ __ __ __ __

__ __ __ __ __ .

PROVERBS 23:22

What makes your dad special?

Write words that describe your dad on the ties.
Then color the picture and give it to him.

Joash, the Boy King (From 2 Chronicles 22:10—23:16)

Ever since he was a baby, Joash had been hidden in the temple.
His bad grandmother killed his family so she could be queen.

Connect the dots.

His aunt and uncle took good care of him.
When Joash was 7 years old, his uncle said something important. What was it?

Write the words in the shapes that match.

The [crown] shall [throne] as the [key].

2 Chronicles 23: 3

reign

king's

promised

son

Lord

Joash's uncle put a crown on his head.
Then everyone shouted, "Long live the king!"

Circle the hidden pictures: trumpet, rose, Bible, ring, sword, cross, bird

The bad queen was killed. King Joash sat on the throne
in the palace. His uncle helped him to be a good king who obeyed God.

Draw a picture of King Joash.

We Are Free! (From Romans 6:15-23)

Every year our country celebrates freedom. We call this Independence Day.

Circle the hidden letters. Then put them in the correct order to read the word.

Jesus wants us to be free too! When we don't know Jesus,
we are the slaves of something very bad. What is it?

Color the spaces with dots to read the word.

But when we love Jesus and live for Him, Jesus saves us! What does the Bible say?
Use the code to find out.

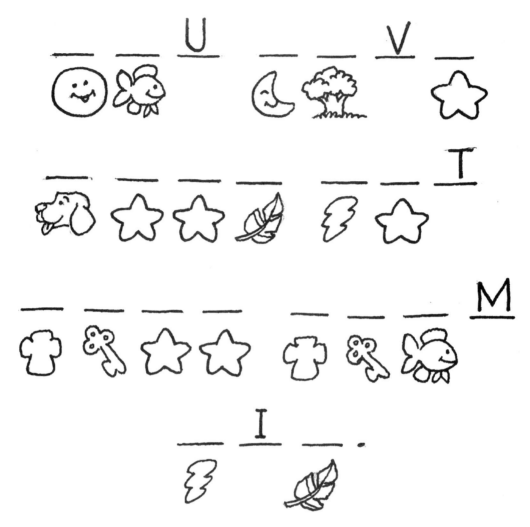

_Y_ _O_ U   _H_ _A_ V _E_

_B_ _E_ _E_ _N_ _S_ _E_ T

_F_ _R_ _E_ _E_ _F_ _R_ _O_ M

_S_ _N_ I .

ROMANS 6:18

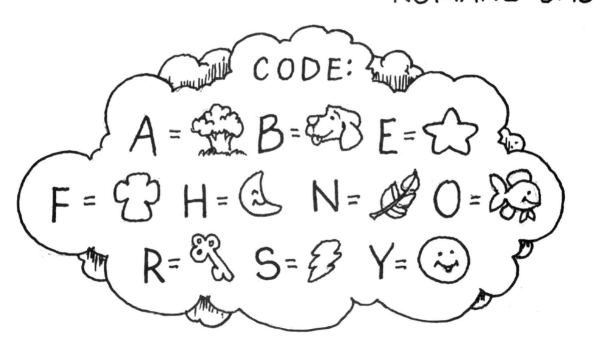

CODE:
A = (tree)   B = (dog)   E = (star)
F = (shirt)   H = (moon)   N = (leaf)   O = (fish)
R = (key)   S = (lightning)   Y = (smiley)

Jesus takes our sins away. Then He promises us life forever in heaven. What are some other great things that happen when you live for Jesus?

Write them in the stripes on the flag. Then color the picture.

The Story of Jonah (From Jonah 1—3)

Jonah didn't want to obey God. "I'll get on a ship and sail away," he thought.

Put an X on 5 things Jonah will NOT need on his trip.

Then a big storm came! Jonah said, "Throw me in the water." So the sailors did.

What happened next? Use the code to find out.

THE LORD
7 19 22 15 12 9 23

SENT A HUGE
8 22 13 7 26 19 6 20 22

FISH TO
21 18 8 19 7 12

SWALLOW
8 4 26 15 15 12 4

JONAH.
17 12 13 26 19

FROM JONAH 2:1

CODE:

A	B	C	D	E	F	G	H	I	J	K	L	M
26	25	24	23	22	21	20	19	18	17	16	15	14

N	O	P	Q	R	S	T	U	V	W	X	Y	Z
13	12	11	10	9	8	7	6	5	4	3	2	1

Jonah knew he should have obeyed. He prayed and God forgave him.
Then the fish spit Jonah out, and he went to preach to the people.

Help Jonah reach the city.

START ▷

Have you ever had a time when you did not want to obey? What happened?

Draw a picture about it here.

Would-Be Followers (From Luke 9:57-62)

Jesus and His disciples were walking along the road.
A man came up and said something to Jesus. What did He say?

Use the code on the clock to find out.

__ __ __ __ __
5 11 5 6 6

__ __ __ __ __ __ __ __ __
2 7 6 6 7 11 1 7 8

__ __ __ __ __ __ __ __
11 4 12 9 12 10 12 9

__ __ __ __ __ .
1 7 8 3 7   LUKE 9:57

Jesus knew life was hard for His followers. He said, "Foxes have holes and birds have nests, but I don't have a place to lay my head."

Circle the hidden pictures: fox, cross, bird, pillow, apple, Bible, shoe, hat

**Later on, a man said he would follow Jesus after his father died.
Another man said, "I need to say goodbye to my family first."**

Which path will lead the men to Jesus?

Jesus said, "No one who puts his <u>hand</u> to the <u>plow</u> and <u>looks</u> back is <u>fit</u> for <u>service</u> in the <u>kingdom</u> of <u>God</u>" (Luke 9:62). Jesus doesn't want us to <u>wait</u>. He wants us to <u>follow</u> Him today!

Circle the underlined words in the puzzle.

Three Men in a Furnace (From Daniel 3)

The king was so mad! He wanted everyone to worship his new statue, but three men would not obey. Who were they?

Write the first letter of each picture to read the names.

The three men said, "Your Majesty, we will not serve
your gods or worship your idol."

Circle the hidden pictures: crown, Bible, necklace, fire, cross, sheep, angel, banana

"If you will not obey me, I will have you thrown in a fiery furnace!" yelled the king. And that is what he did.

Connect the dots.

The fire was very hot, but the men did not burn up!
The king saw FOUR men in the furnace. Maybe the fourth man was an angel or the
Son of God. God saved Shadrach, Meshach, and Abednego!

Draw the fourth man in the furnace.

The Good Samaritan (From Luke 10:25-37)

A hurt man was lying on the road. Robbers took his money and clothes.
Then they beat him up.

Put an X on 5 things that do not belong in the picture.

Three men passed by, but only one was kind enough to help the hurt man.

Who was it? *Solve the maze to find out.*

The Good Samaritan bandaged the man's cuts. He poured oil and wine on them. Then he put the man on his donkey and took him to the inn.

Number the pictures in order from 1-4.

**Jesus wants us to love our neighbor and be kind to people in trouble.
The Good Samaritan was a neighbor to the hurt man. How?**

Write the letter BEFORE the letter under the line to find out.

—	—		—	—	—
I	F		I	B	E

—	—	—	—	—
N	F	S	D	Z

—	—	—	—	—
P	O	I	J	N

FROM LUKE 10:37

ABCDEFGHIJKLM
NOPQRSTUVWXYZ

Daniel in the Lions' Den (From Daniel 6)

The king was very worried! Bad men had asked him to make a bad law.
What was it? *Use the code to find out.*

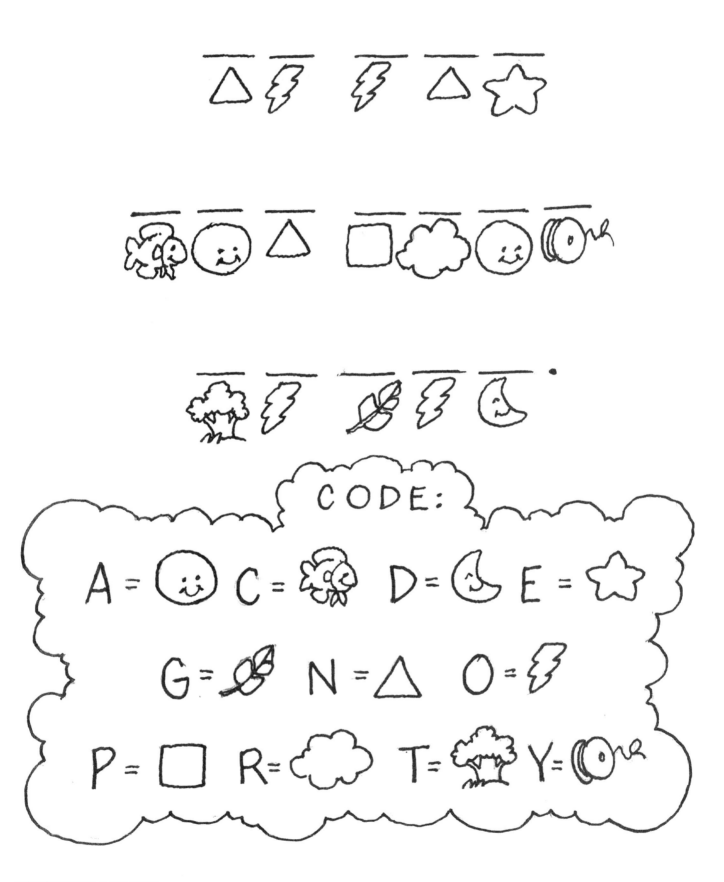

CODE:

A = (smiley) C = (fish) D = (moon) E = (star)

G = (leaf) N = (triangle) O = (lightning)

P = (square) R = (cloud) T = (tree) Y = (yoyo)

**Anyone who prayed to God would be thrown in the lions' den.
The king's friend, Daniel, always prayed to God!**

Draw the lions in the den.

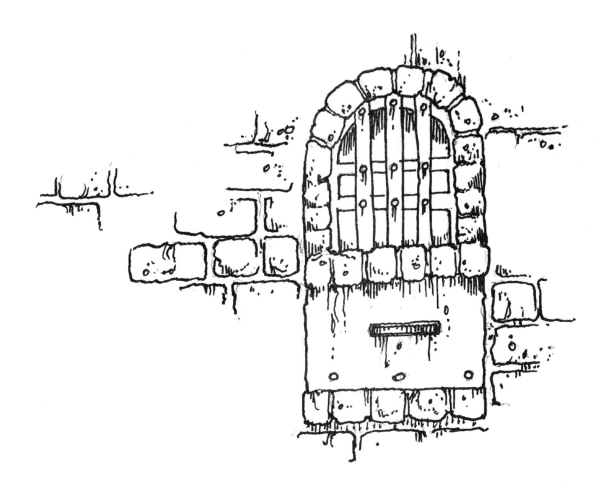

The king did not want to hurt Daniel, but the bad men said,
"You have to obey the law." The sad king said, "Daniel, may your God rescue you!"

Circle the hidden pictures: apple, Bible, crown, butterfly, praying hands, heart, cross, dog

The next morning the king was happy! Daniel was alive!
Who did God send to save Daniel from the lions?

Connect the dots.

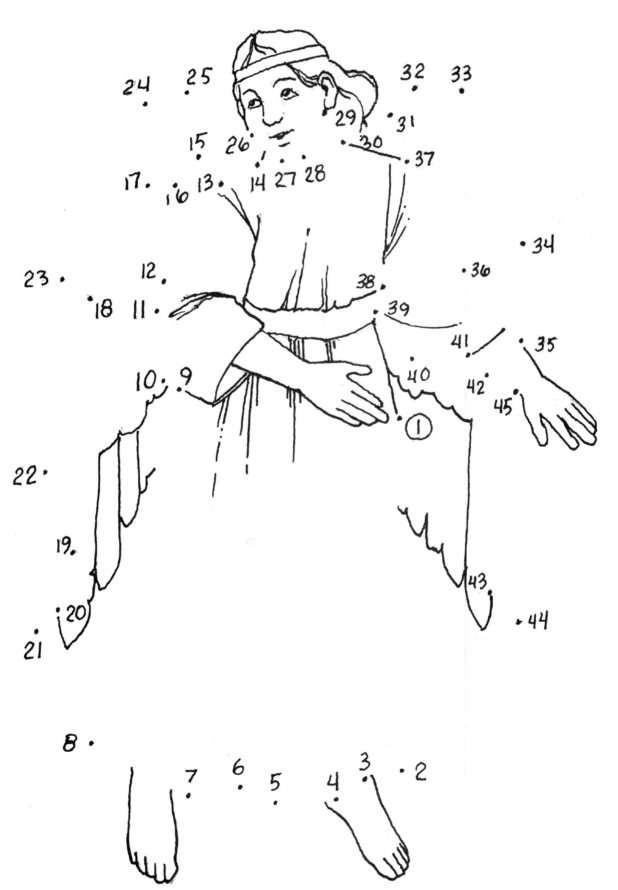

Parable of the Supper (From Luke 14:15-24)

A man wanted to have a big party. He invited lots of people.
Later, he sent them a message. What did it say?

Cross out every K. Then write the letters you have left on the lines.

__ __ __ __ __ __ ,

__ __ __ __ __ __ __ __ __ __ __

__ __ __ __ __ __ . FROM LUKE 14:17

Everyone began making excuses for why they couldn't come to the party.
What did they say? *Write the words in the shapes that match.*

I just [bag shape] a [cloud shape] .

I just [scroll shape] [oxen yoke shape] .

of [horn/oxen shape] .

I just got [heart shape] .

married   bought

5 yoke   field

bought   oxen

The man was mad! He told his servant, "Go <u>quickly</u> to the <u>streets</u> and <u>alleys</u> of the <u>town</u>. Bring the <u>poor</u>, the <u>crippled</u>, the <u>blind</u>, and the <u>lame</u>" (From Luke 14:21).

Put the underlined words where they fit in the crossword puzzle.
Some letters are given to help you.

Soon, people were eating good food and having fun. Just like the man invited everyone to his party, Jesus wants everyone to follow Him. Sadly, not everyone will.

Draw a picture of the party.

Queen Esther (From Esther 2—8)

Esther, a beautiful Jewish girl, had just become queen. No one knew she was a Jew.

Draw Esther's crown.

One day, Esther's cousin Mordecai sent her a message.
A bad man named Haman had a terrible plan. What was it?

Use the code to find out.

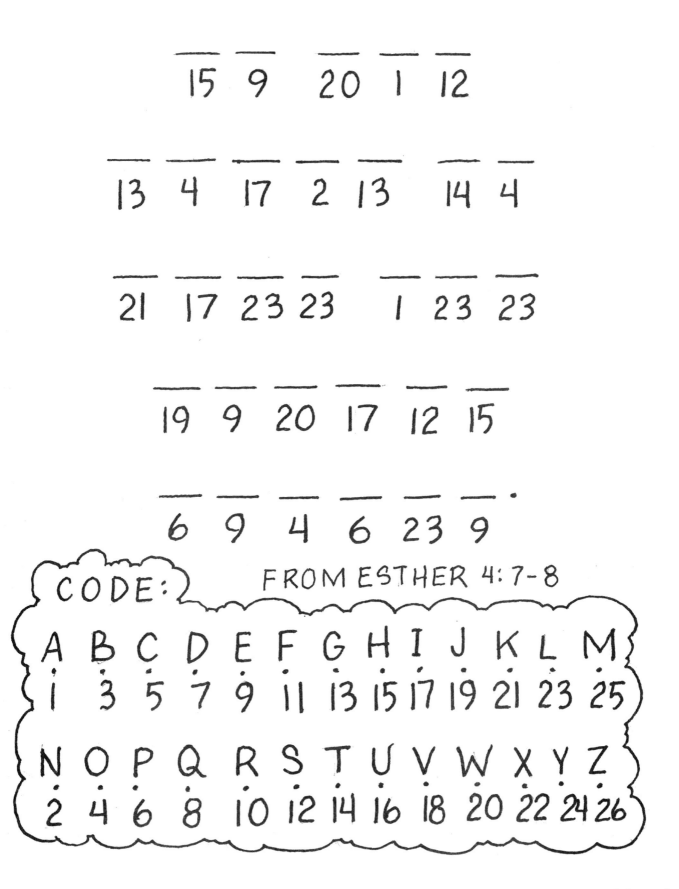

FROM ESTHER 4:7-8

CODE:

A	B	C	D	E	F	G	H	I	J	K	L	M
1	3	5	7	9	11	13	15	17	19	21	23	25

N	O	P	Q	R	S	T	U	V	W	X	Y	Z
2	4	6	8	10	12	14	16	18	20	22	24	26

Mordecai wanted Esther to tell the king.
But Esther knew she could be killed if she went to the king without being invited.
For three days, Esther and her people prayed.

Connect the dots.

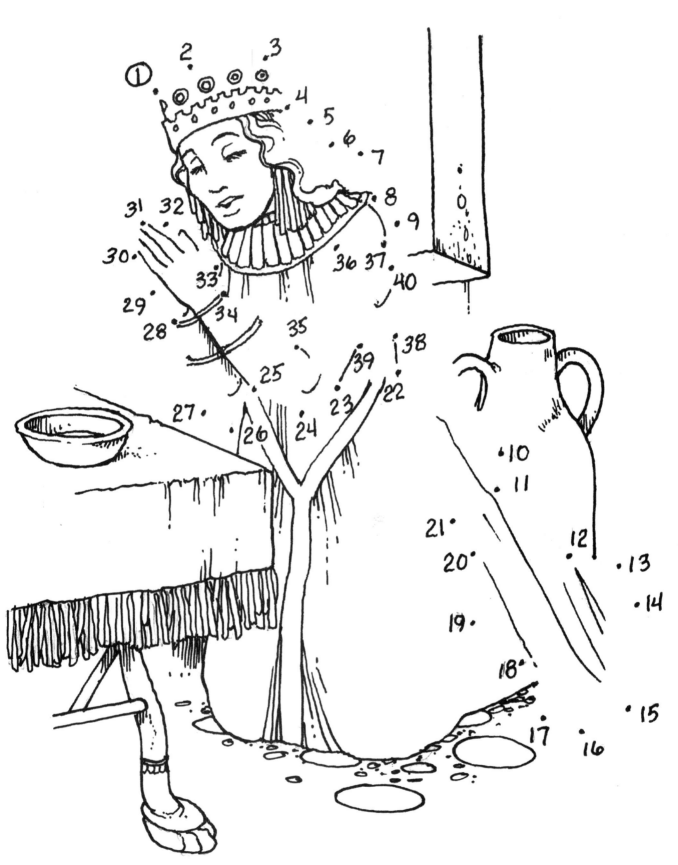

God heard Esther's prayers. The king was kind and saved her people.
All the Jews in the city had a special party because they were so happy.

Circle the hidden pictures: crown, trumpet, Bible, plate, cup, robe, cross, mouse

Two Kinds of Prayers (From Luke 18:9-14)

One day Jesus told a story about two men who prayed.
One was a Pharisee, and the other was a tax collector.

Help the men reach the temple.

The Pharisee prayed, "God, thank You that I am better than other people. I'm not a robber, an evil person, or even like that tax collector over there."

Put an X on 5 things that are wrong with the picture.

The tax collector stood off by himself. He bowed his head sadly. What did he pray?

Mark out every Q and Z. Then write the letters you have left on the lines.

GOD, HAVE

MERCY ON ME,

A SINNER. LUKE 18:13

Who do you think God blessed that day?

Follow the lines from the letters to the boxes. Then write the letters to read the answer.

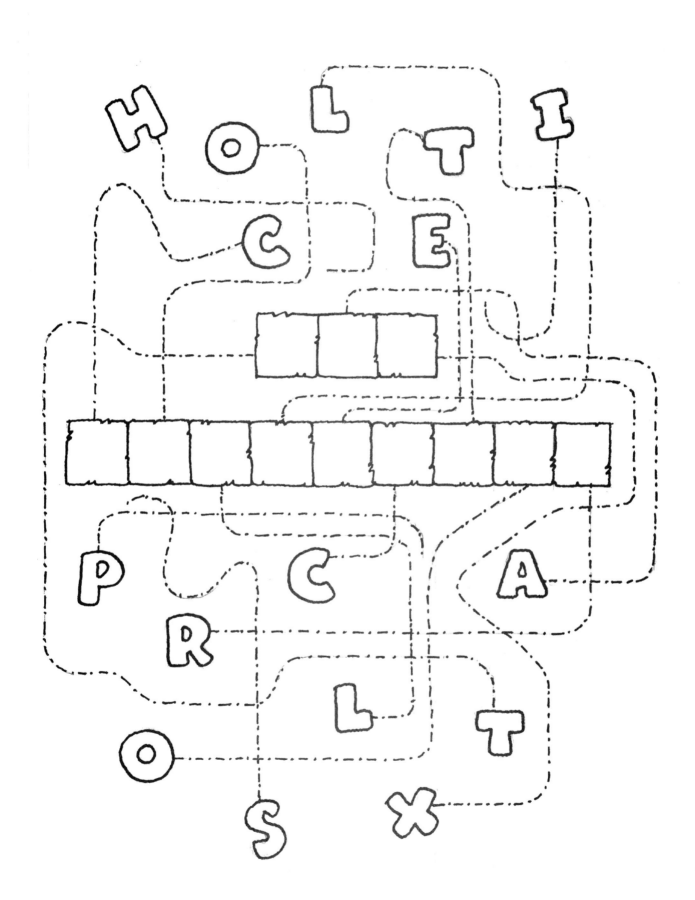

Labor Day

(From Proverbs 30:24-25, 2 Thessalonians 3:6-13, 2 Timothy 2:15)

On Labor Day we celebrate the jobs people do. God is happy when we do good work.

Match the worker with the correct tools.

In the Bible, Paul says God doesn't want us to be lazy.
We shouldn't let others do all the work. What did Paul say people should do?

Write the first letter of each picture to find out.

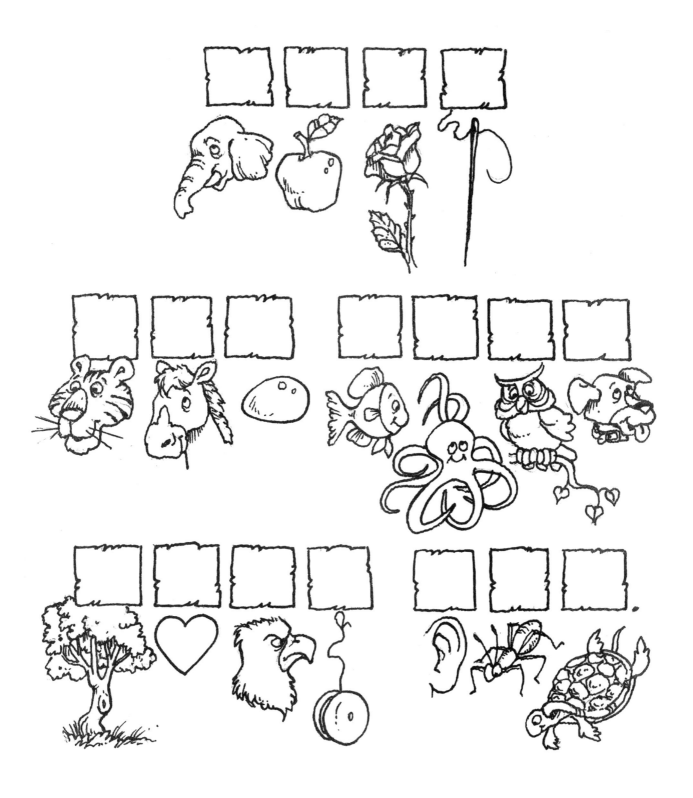

2 THESSALONIANS 3:12

Proverbs 30:24-25 tells about a little creature that is very wise. It works hard to store up food in the summer, so it will have plenty to eat later.

What is it? Connect the dots.

1

30

29 28

2

27

5 4

3

6

26

7

25 8

22 23 24 12 9

13

11 10

21

20

14

19

15

18 17 16

The Bible says, "Do your best to present yourself to God as...a worker who does not need to be ashamed" (2 Timothy 2:15). When we work, God is proud of us!

Draw a picture of a job you can do.

The Tower of Babel (From Genesis 11:1-9)

Long ago, everyone in the world spoke the same language.

Unscramble the letters to find some of the languages people speak today.

..... MAGERN

..... FCHREN

.. GLENISH

.. ISHANSP

One day, the people said, "Let's build something, so everyone will see how great we are." What did they want to build?

Use the code to find out.

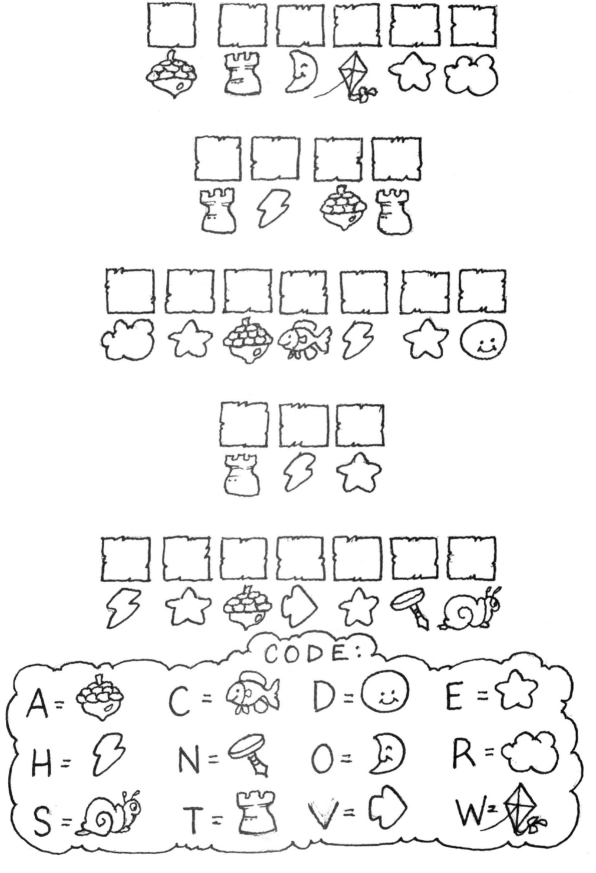

When God saw what they were doing, He was not pleased.

Circle the hidden pictures: hammer, saw, brick, cross, hat, Bible, spider, comb

God mixed up their **language**, so the **people** couldn't **speak** the same one anymore.
They stopped **building** the **tower** and **moved** away from each other,
all around the **world**.

Put the underlined words where they fit in the crossword puzzle.
Some letters are given to help you.

Doubting Thomas (From John 20:24-31)

"Thomas! We have some exciting news!" said the disciples. What was it?

Write the first letter of each picture to find out.

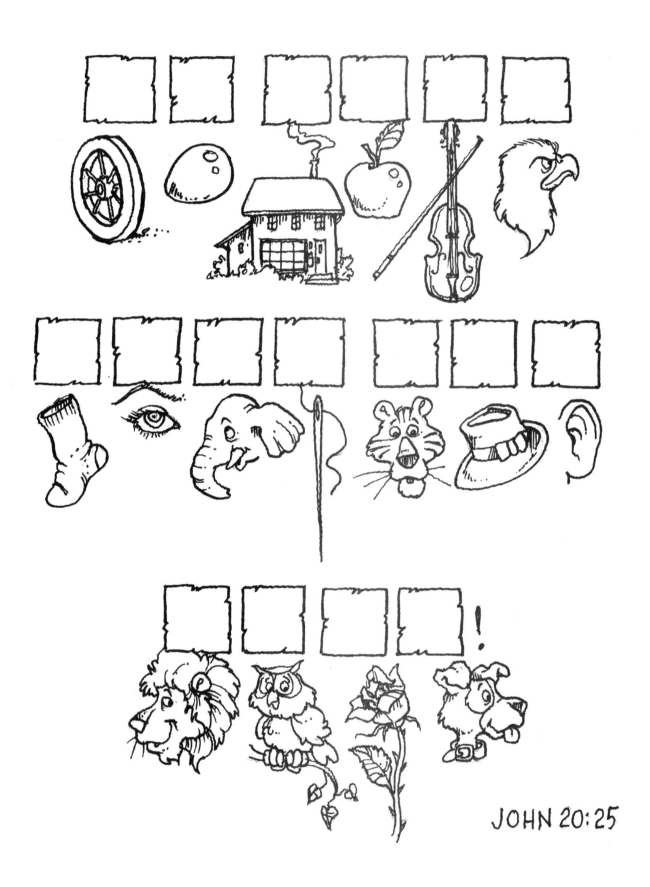

JOHN 20:25

Thomas didn't believe them. He knew Jesus had died.
"Unless I see the nail marks in his hands and put my finger where the nails were,
and put my hand into his side, I will not believe," he said. (John 20:25)

Circle the words in the puzzle.

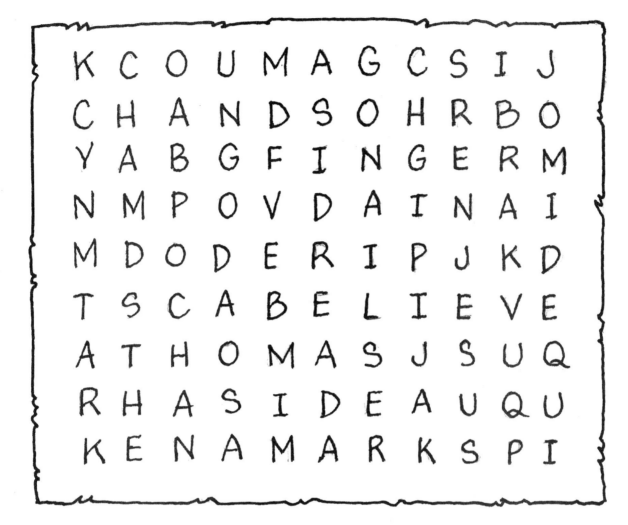

K C O U M A G C S I J
C H A N D S O H R B O
Y A B G F I N G E R M
N M P O V D A I N A I
M D O D E R I P J K D
T S C A B E L I E V E
A T H O M A S J S U Q
R H A S I D E A U Q U
K E N A M A R K S P I

A week later, Thomas and the other disciples were in a house. The doors were locked. Suddenly someone appeared in the room. Who was it?

Connect the dots.

Thomas touched Jesus' scars. Jesus really was alive!
Jesus said, "You believe because you see Me. People will be blessed
if they believe without seeing Me first" (from John 20:29).

Circle the hidden pictures:
frog, eyeglasses, nail, hammer, cross, magnifying glass, Bible, flashlight

Nehemiah (From Nehemiah 1—12)

Nehemiah was the king's cupbearer. He made sure
the king's wine was safe for him to drink.

Color in the spaces with dots to see the picture.

One day the king asked, "Nehemiah, why are you sad?" Nehemiah said,
"The walls and gates of Jerusalem have been destroyed."
The king said he could go and help fix them.

Help Nehemiah reach Jerusalem.

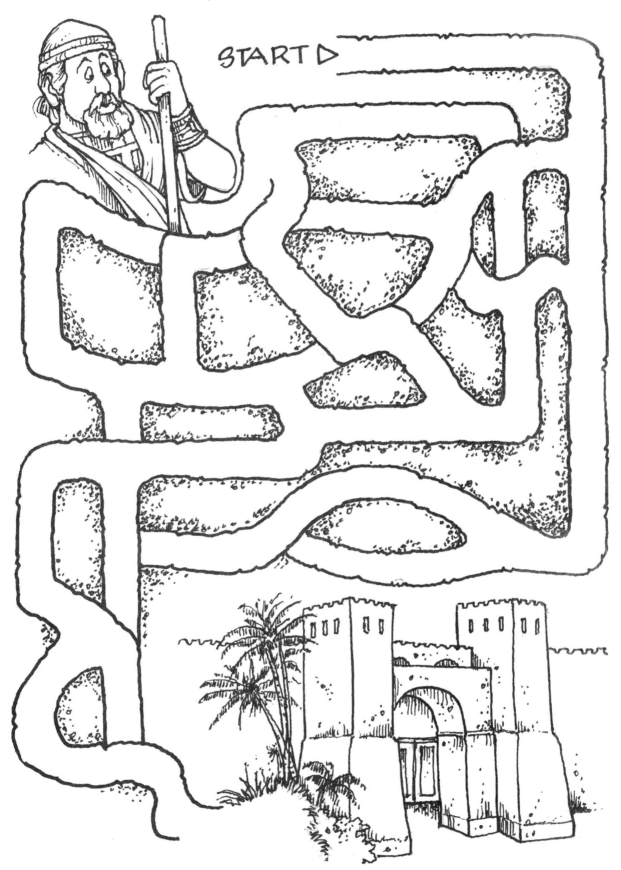

Nehemiah met with the city leaders. What did he say?

Write the letter that comes BEFORE the letter under the line to find out.

,
‾ ‾ ‾ ‾
M F U T

‾ ‾ ‾ ‾ ‾ ‾ ‾
S F C V J M E

‾ ‾ ‾ ‾ ‾ ‾ ‾ ‾ ‾
U I F X B M M P G

‾ ‾ ‾ ‾ ‾ ‾ ‾ ‾ ‾
K F S V T B M F N .

NEHEMIAH 2:17

A B C D E F G H I J K L M
N O P Q R S T U V W X Y Z

**When they were done, they dedicated the wall to God.
They sang joyful songs and celebrated all that God had done for them.**

Draw a picture of the happy people.

Jesus Returns to Heaven (From Acts 1:1-11)

After Jesus rose from the tomb, He appeared to His followers.
He talked and ate with them.

Circle the hidden pictures: Bible, fish, bread, grapes, apple, fork, spoon, cross

Jesus said, "Don't leave Jerusalem. Wait for the gift God has promised." What was the gift?

Write the first letter of each picture in the boxes to find out.

When Jesus finished talking, He went up to heaven in the clouds.

Connect the dots.

The men were looking up into the sky.
Suddenly, two angels dressed in white stood next to them. What did they say?
Use the code to find out.

19 9 12 16 12 20 17 23 23
JESUS WILL

5 4 25 9 3 1 5 21
COME BACK

14 15 9 12 1 25 9
THE SAME

20 1 24 15 9 20 9 2 14
WAY HE WENT

14 4 15 9 1 18 9 2.
TO HEAVEN.

ACTS 1:11

CODE:

A	B	C	D	E	F	G	H	I	J	K	L	M
1	3	5	7	9	11	13	15	17	19	21	23	25

N	O	P	Q	R	S	T	U	V	W	X	Y	Z
2	4	6	8	10	12	14	16	18	20	22	24	26

Gideon Fights a Battle (From Judges 7)

Gideon took 32,000 men to fight the enemy army. What did God say?

Use the code to find out.

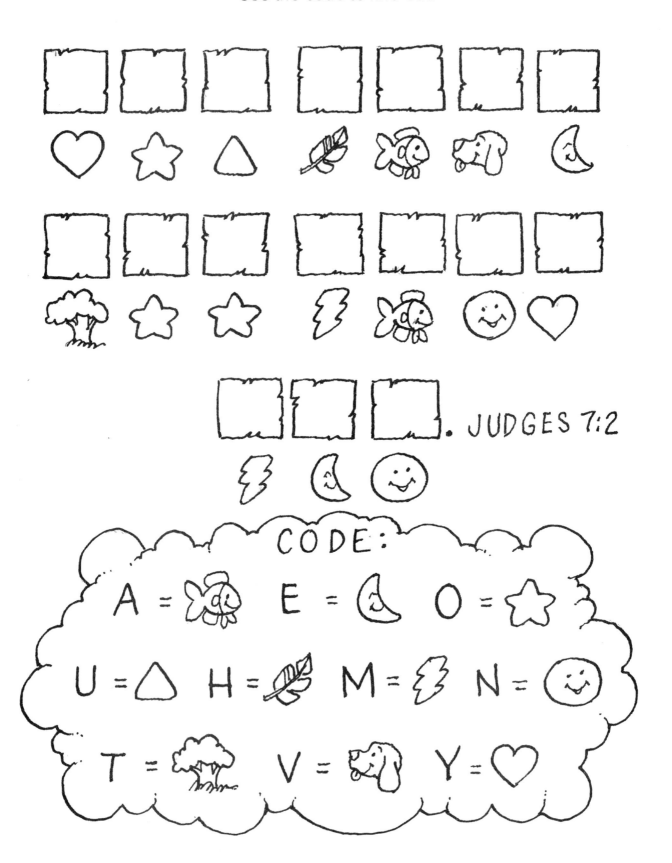

. JUDGES 7:2

God told Gideon to send some men home. How many were left?

Color in the spaces with dots to find out.

God promised to help Gideon. He and his servant spied on the enemy camp. They heard a man say Gideon would win the battle.

Help Gideon find his way to the camp.

Gideon said, "Bring trumpets and jars with torches inside them."
When they played the trumpets and smashed their jars, the enemy ran away!

Put an X on 5 things that are wrong with the picture.

Saul on the Damascus Road (From Acts 9:1-8)

Saul hated Christians. He wanted to throw them all in jail.

Which path leads to the jail?

Saul was on the road to Damascus when a bright light appeared. He heard a voice say, "Saul, Saul, why do you persecute Me?" Who was it?

Circle the letters J-E-S-U-S hidden in the picture.

Jesus told Saul to go into the city. When Saul got up, he had a big problem. What was it? *Write the letter that comes BEFORE the letter under the line.*

‾‾ ‾‾ ‾‾ ‾‾ ‾‾ ‾‾ ‾‾ ‾‾
I F P Q F O F E

‾‾ ‾‾ ‾‾ ‾‾ ‾‾ ‾‾ ‾‾
I J T F Z F T

‾‾ ‾‾ ‾‾ ‾‾ ‾‾ ‾‾ ‾‾ ‾‾
C V U D P V M E

‾‾ ‾‾ ‾‾ ‾‾ ‾‾ ‾‾
O P U T F F

A B C D E F G H I J K L M
N O P Q R S T U V W X Y Z

Later, the Lord sent Ananias to heal Saul's eyes.
Then Saul began to preach the good news about Jesus.

Draw a picture of Saul here.

The Sun and Moon Stand Still (From Joshua 10:1-15)

The king of Jerusalem was worried. The people of Gibeon and Israel had made peace. He sent a message to four kings. What was it?

Use the code to find out.

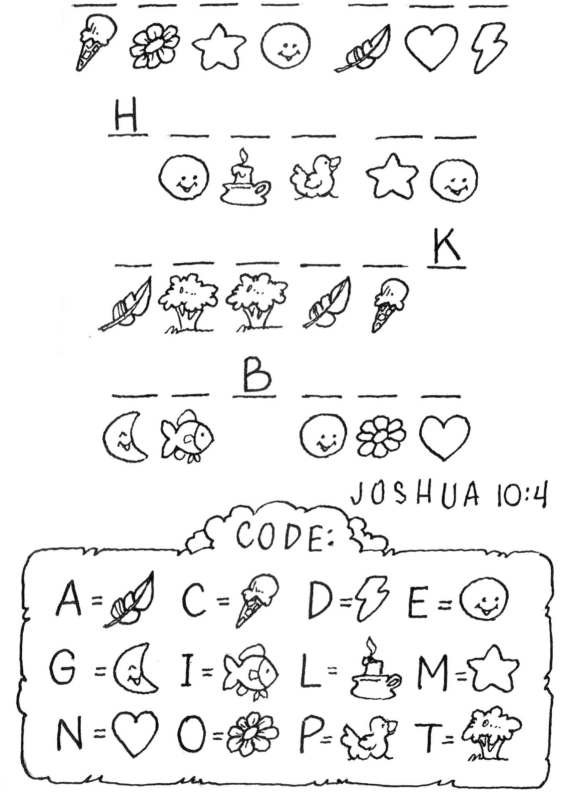

The people of Gibeon saw the kings' men coming to fight.
They asked Joshua to help them.

Help Joshua and his army reach Gibeon.

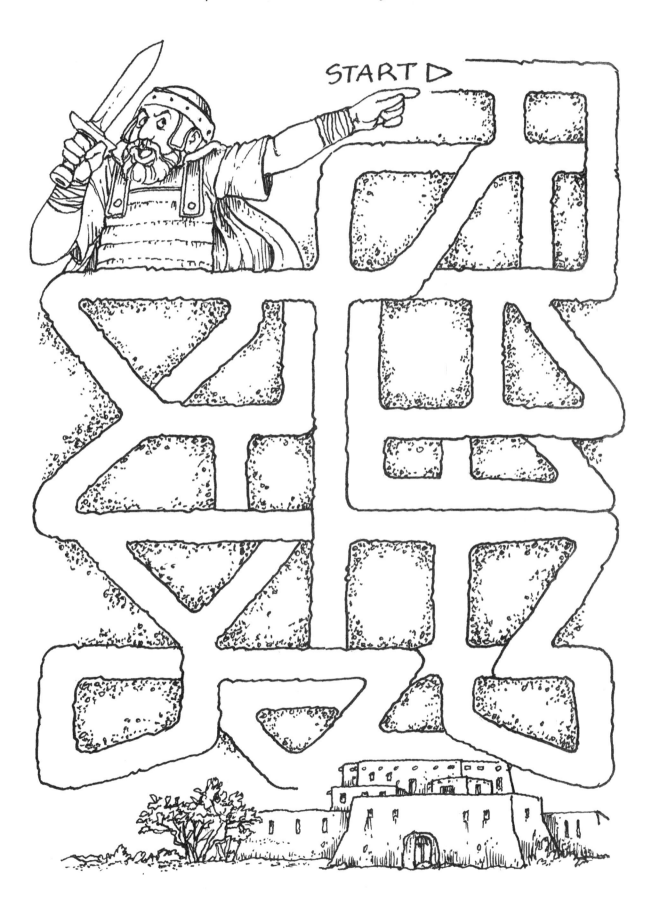

The men fought, and Israel and Gibeon won. Joshua did not want
any enemies to escape. He said, "Sun, stand still over Gibeon,
and you, moon, over the Valley of Aijalon."

Circle the hidden pictures: sword, feather, sun, moon, Bible, cross, crown, bird

‾ ‾ ‾ ‾ ‾ ‾
7 19 22 8 6 13

‾ ‾ ‾ ‾ ‾
8 7 12 12 23

‾ ‾ ‾ ‾ ‾ ‾ ‾ ‾
8 7 18 15 15 26 13 23

‾ ‾ ‾ ‾ ‾ ‾ ‾
7 19 22 14 12 12 13

‾ ‾ ‾ ‾ ‾ ‾ ‾ .
8 7 12 11 11 22 23

JOSHUA 10:13

CODE:

A	B	C	D	E	F	G	H	I	J	K	L	M
26	25	24	23	22	21	20	19	18	17	16	15	14

N	O	P	Q	R	S	T	U	V	W	X	Y	Z
13	12	11	10	9	8	7	6	5	4	3	2	1

Peter and Cornelius (From Acts 10:23-48)

Cornelius was a good man who loved God. He also helped poor people.

Connect the dots.

One day Cornelius was praying. He wanted to learn more about God. Suddenly, someone came and told him to send for Peter. Who was it?

Follow the lines from the letters to the boxes. Then write the letters to read the name.

Peter was a Jew and Cornelius was a Gentile. Usually, Jews didn't visit Gentiles. But God told Peter it was the right thing to do. What did Peter say?

Cross out every K and Z. Then write the letters you have left on the lines.

START

_ _ _
ACCEPTS

_ _ _ _ _ _ _ _ _ _ WHO _ _ _ _

_ _ _ IS _ _ _ _ _ - ACTS 10:34-35

Cornelius had invited many people to his house to meet Peter. They were so glad to learn about Jesus! Who will you tell about Jesus?

Draw their picture here.

Deborah Leads God's People (From Judges 4)

Deborah was a prophet and judge in Israel.
She told the people what God wanted them to know.

Connect the dots.

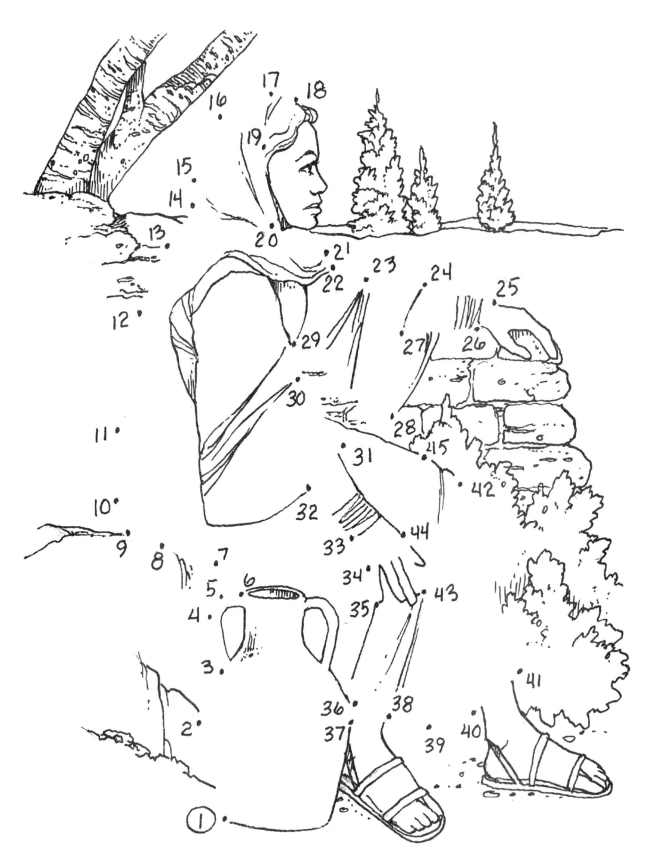

One day, Deborah sent for Barak. "God wants you to take your army to fight our enemies," she said. What did Barak say?

Write the letter that comes AFTER the letter under the line.

‾ ‾   ‾ ‾ ‾   ‾ ‾
H E   X N T   F N

‾ ‾ ‾ ‾   ‾ ‾'
V H S G   L D

‾   ‾ ‾ ‾ ‾   ‾ ‾.
H   V H K K   F N

JUDGES 4:8

ABCDEFGHIJKLM
NOPQRSTUVWXYZ

Deborah said, "I will go too." Barak and his men would fight, but a woman would defeat the enemy. What do the men need for the battle?

Circle the correct items. Put an X on things they don't need.

The enemy's leader ran away. He hid in a woman's tent, and she killed him. Deborah's words came true. What brave woman killed the enemy?

Follow the lines from the letters to the boxes. Then write the letters to read her name.

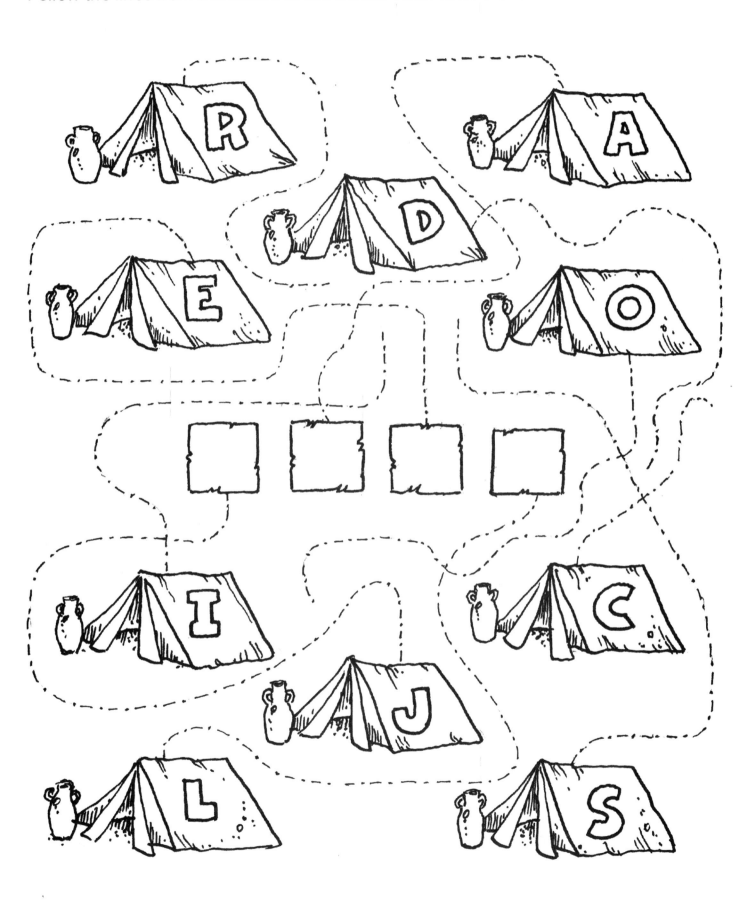

Paul Is Shipwrecked (From Acts 27)

Paul was a prisoner. He had to go on a ship to Rome. *Draw Paul's chains.*

Soon, the ship was caught in a bad storm. The men were afraid the ship would sink. They threw the cargo into the sea.

Circle the hidden pictures: anchor, fish, Bible, rope, fishing pole, seagull, starfish, cross

Paul had a message from God. "The ship will be lost, but no one will die."
What else did Paul say? *Write the words in the shapes that match.*

UP YOUR ☁, △. I HAVE ♥ IN ☀.

ACTS 27:25

GOD · KEEP · COURAGE · FAITH · MEN

When the ship was close to land, Paul prayed and everyone ate.
Then some men swam, and others floated to shore holding boards.
Everyone was safe! How many men were saved?

Color in the spaces with dots to find out.

Are You Thankful? (From Psalm 136)

God does so much for us! He gives us food to eat, clothes to wear,
a home, and people who love us. *What should we say to God?*

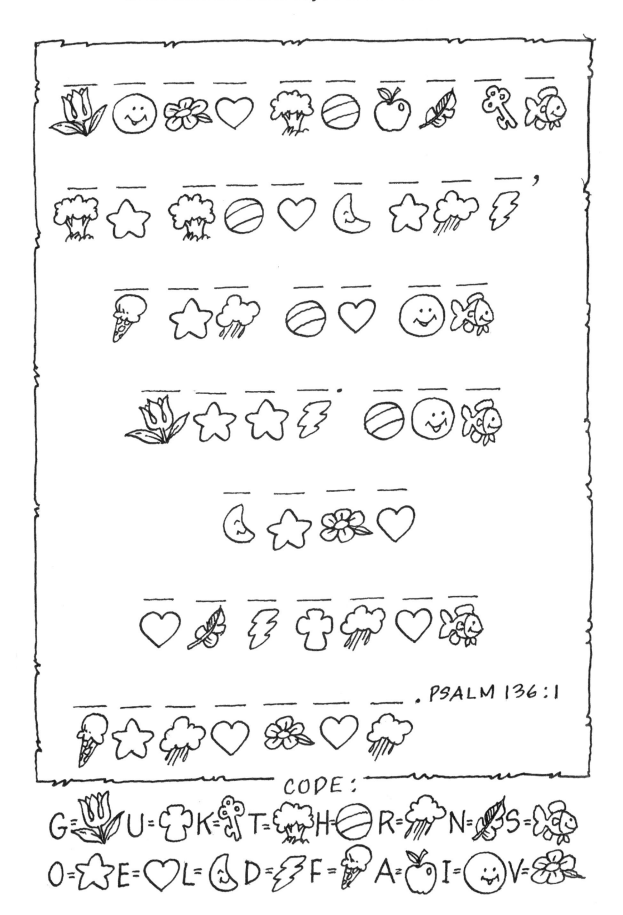

CODE:

PSALM 136:1

Many people spend time with family and friends at Thanksgiving. They may enjoy a special meal together.

Help the kids reach their grandma's house in time for dinner.

How many words can you make from the letters below?

John Sees a Vision (From Revelation 1:9-20)

When he was younger, John was Jesus' disciple.
Now he was old and lived on an island. He was a prisoner. Why?

Write the first letter of each picture to find out.

One day, John had a vision. A vision is like a dream that God uses to show or tell us something important.

Circle the hidden pictures: star, candle, sword, Bible, sun, cross, dove, trumpet

In the vision John saw 7 gold lampstands.
He also saw someone dressed in a long robe with a gold sash. Who was it?
Connect the dots.

John **wrote** down the **important** things **Jesus** told him.
Later, he had a **vision** about **heaven** too.
We can read about it in the last Book of the **Bible**, **Revelation**.

Find and circle the underlined words in the puzzle.

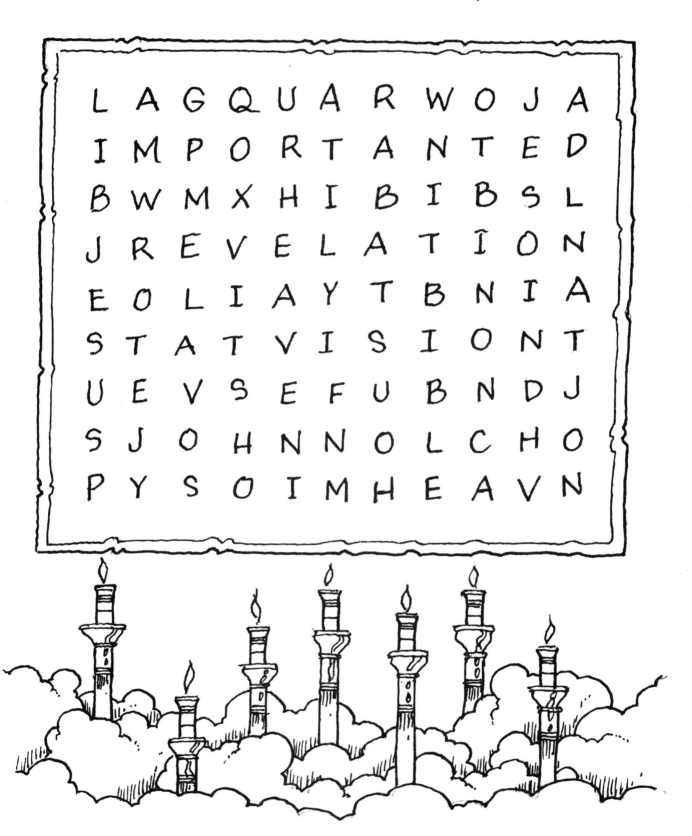

L A G Q U A R W O J A
I M P O R T A N T E D
B W M X H I B I B S L
J R E V E L A T I O N
E O L I A Y T B N I A
S T A T V I S I O N T
U E V S E F U B N D J
S J O H N N O L C H O
P Y S O I M H E A V N

Christmas Songs (From Luke 2:14)

When Christmas time is here, we like to sing special songs.
What is another word for song?

Follow the lines from the notes to the boxes. Then write the letters.

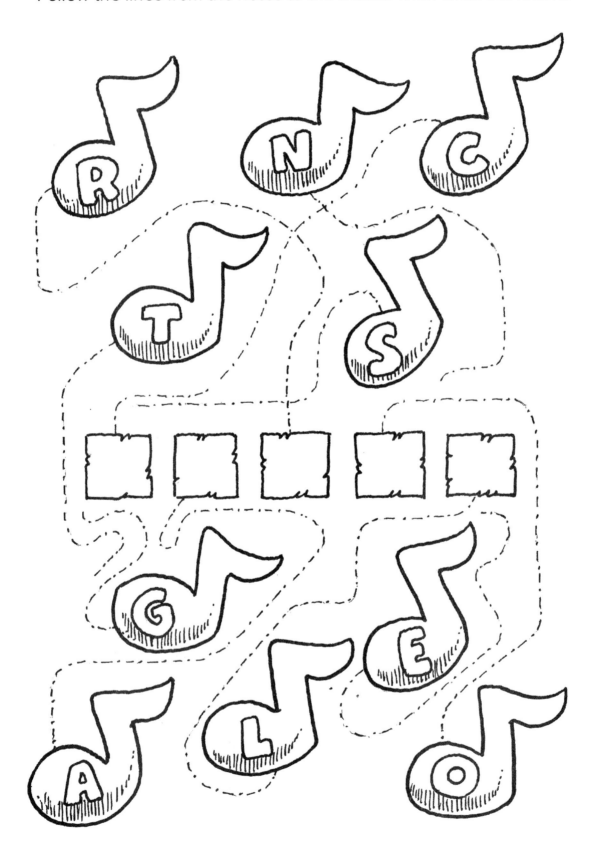

Many songs we sing at church tell the story of Jesus' birth.
We want to share that good news with everyone!

Draw a line from the song to the picture that matches.

Away in a Manger

Go, Tell It on the Mountain

O Little Town of Bethlehem

Hark! The Herald Angels Sing

We Three Kings of Orient Are

Christmas songs help us praise God. Long ago, angels praised God when Jesus was born. What did the angels say?

Use the code to find out.

13 23 4 10 24 14 4
(G L O R Y T O)

13 4 7 17 2 14 15 9
(G O D I N T H E)

15 17 13 15 9 12 14
(H I G H E S T)

15 9 1 18 9 2
(H E A V E N)

LUKE 2:14

CODE:

A	B	C	D	E	F	G	H	I	J	K	L	M
1	3	5	7	9	11	13	15	17	19	21	23	25

N	O	P	Q	R	S	T	U	V	W	X	Y	Z
2	4	6	8	10	12	14	16	18	20	22	24	26

What is your favorite Christmas song? *Draw a picture of you singing for Jesus!*

Christmas Bible Verses (From Luke 2:8-20)

The Bible tells us the wonderful story of Jesus' birth.
One night, shepherds were out in the fields, watching their sheep.

Connect the dots.

**An <u>angel</u> came! He said, "Do not be <u>afraid</u>.
I <u>bring</u> you <u>good</u> <u>news</u> that will cause <u>great</u> <u>joy</u> for all <u>people</u>" (Luke 2:10).**

Put the underlined words in the grid where they belong.

What else did the angel say?

Write the letter that comes BEFORE the letter under the line.
Then read the Bible verse.

U P E B Z
IN THE ____ OF
U P X O

____ A
E B W J E

T B W J P S I B T
____ TO
C F F O C P S O

____ ; ____ THE
Z P V I F J T

____ , THE
N F T T J B I

____ . ____ 2:11
M P S E M V L F

A B C D E F G H I J K L M
N O P Q R S T U V W X Y Z

Then the angel told them where to find Baby Jesus.
"You will find a baby wrapped in cloths and lying in a manger" (Luke 2:12).

Put an X on 5 things that do not belong in the picture.

Christmas Traditions (From Luke 2:31, Matthew 2:11)

A tradition is something special we do to celebrate an important day.
Does your family have any Christmas traditions?

Draw decorations on the Christmas tree.

Many people read the Christmas story in the Bible. They want to remember why we celebrate. In the Bible what did the angel say to Mary?

Cross out every P and Q. Then write the letters you have left on the lines.

START

YOU _ _ _ _ _ _ _ _

_ _ _ _ _ _ TO A _ _ _

AND YOU _ _ _ _ _

_ _ _ _ _ _ _ _ _ _ .

LUKE 1:31

We often give gifts to people we love at Christmas.
The wise men brought Jesus 3 special gifts. What were they?

Write the first letter of each picture in the box to find out.

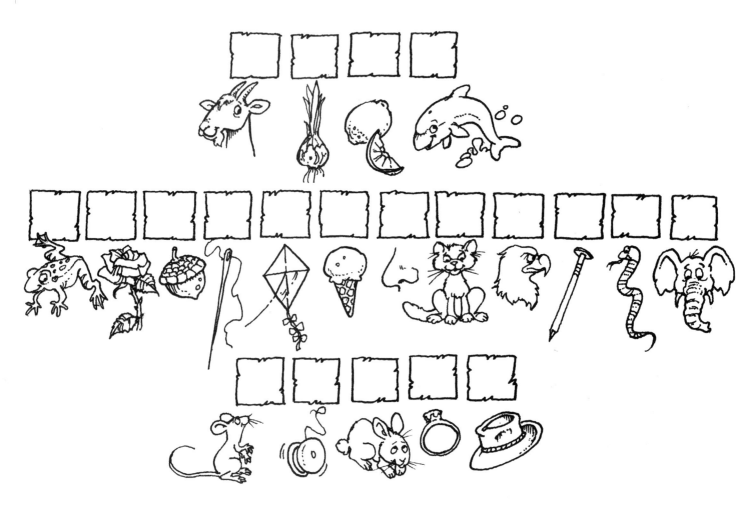

Unscramble the words to find some more Christmas traditions.
Then draw a line to match the words to the correct picture.

Bake okiscoe
_ _ _ _ _ _ _

Sing rolcas
_ _ _ _ _ _

Give figts
_ _ _ _ _

Visit lymiaf
_ _ _ _ _ _

Read the lebBi
_ _ _ _ _

Jesus Is Here! (From Luke 2)

Mary and Joseph had to go on a long trip to Bethlehem.

Which path leads to Bethlehem?

When they got to town, there was no place for them to stay.
An innkeeper let them stay in his stable.

Circle the hidden pictures: baby bottle, Bible, teddy bear, cross, bib, rattle, bowl, spoon

In the stable, Mary gave birth to God's Son, Jesus. She had no bed for the baby, so she put him in something that held hay for the animals. What was this called?

Follow the lines from the letters to the boxes. Write the letters to read the words.